for Gifted Students

College Planning
for Gifted Students

Choosing and Getting
Into the Right College

Sandra L. Berger

PRUFROCK PRESS INC.
WACO, TEXAS

Copyright © 2006 Prufrock Press Inc.

Edited by Lacy Elwood
Graphic Production by Kim Worley
Cover Design by Marjorie Parker

ISBN-13 978-1-59363-181-9
ISBN-10 1-59363-181-2

Berger, Sandra L.
  College planning for gifted students : choosing and getting into the right
college / Sandra Berger.—3rd ed.
    p. cm.
  Includes bibliographical references.
  ISBN 1-59363-181-2 (pbk.)
  1. College choice—United States. 2. Gifted children—Education—United
States. 3. College student orientation—United States. I. Title.
  LB2350.5.B47 2006
  371.95'74—dc22
                          2006005108

Printed in the United States of America.

At the time of this book's publication, all facts and figures cited are the most current available. All telephone numbers, addresses, and Web site URLs are accurate and active. All publications, organizations, Web sites, and other resources exist as described in the book, and all have been verified. The authors and Prufrock Press Inc., make no warranty or guarantee concerning the information and materials given out by organizations or content found at Web sites, and we are not responsible for any changes that occur after this book's publication. If you find an error, please contact Prufrock Press Inc.

Prufrock Press Inc.
P.O. Box 8813
Waco, TX 76714-8813
Phone: (800) 998-2208
Fax: (800) 240-0333
http://www.prufrock.com

To my wonderful gifted daughters, Bonnie Proctor, Judy Reese, and Deb Berger, who inspired this book.

Table of Contents

Acknowledgements

College Planning for Gifted Students, written by a parent and long-time advocate for gifted children, is the product of many efforts. Numerous administrators, counselors, teachers, parents, and students were interviewed for and contributed to this book. The author expresses sincere appreciation to the individuals listed below and to the many students and adults who, over the years, contributed indirectly by speaking freely about their concerns and experiences. Last, but certainly not least, I very much appreciate the efforts of the energetic and creative people at Prufrock Press, especially Lacy Elwood, editor. Special thanks goes to Dorothy Knopper, Open Space Communications, who read early versions and made helpful suggestions.

The author would like to thank the following contributors:

- The parent of a learning-disabled child and a former homeschool student for telling their stories, which became the basis for the vignettes in the sections on students with learning disabilities and homeschooling students.
- The section on career centers was prepared with the assistance of Laurie Kobick, College/Career Center Resource Specialist, Thomas Jefferson High School for Science and Technology, Fairfax, VA.

- Guidelines for writing a teacher recommendation were contributed by Bernis von zur Muehlen, James Madison High School, Fairfax County Public Schools, VA.
- Guidelines for writing a college application essay were contributed by Gail Hubbard, Prince William County Public Schools, Manassas, VA.
- The section on college costs was contributed by Joseph Re, Executive Vice President, Octameron Associates, Alexandria, VA.
- The Student Questionnaire: Why Are You Going to College? (p. 50) and questions you may want to ask during the college interview (p. 162) were based on the work of Shirley Levin, an independent college counselor.

College Planning

College planning is a major event in the lives of many families. Some parents dress their infants in tiny clothing bearing their alma mater's colors and mascots, certain that someday, their child will follow in their footsteps. Other families claim to "bleed" maroon, burnt orange, navy blue and gold, or crimson red, with generations of family members attending the same university. Across the nation, longtime rivalries are upheld during football and basketball season, and carried over to friendly game-day disputes between siblings, friends, or neighbors who chose to attend competing universities. Only in America is the decal from almost any college displayed proudly on the rear window of the family car.

The hopes and dreams of many American families are connected to a college education. We are surrounded by reminders of higher education—everything from ads for college financing, to slick TV descriptions of the competing universities during halftime at the fall football games on Saturday afternoons, to a TV series about a rock star finally going to college. In the 21st century, attending college is part of the American success story.

High school students and their parents often have strong feelings about attending, or not attending college, but once the decision is made to go, choosing the *right* college becomes a different matter altogether. The path from secondary to higher education is poorly marked. Students surveyed for this book said that trying to select a college is confusing, because there is no sound basis for making a decision. They felt overwhelmed by the amount of mail they received from colleges each day featuring sports, special programs, and stately granite buildings set on idyllic grassy knolls or downtown in bustling cities. Each brochure seems to say, "Choose me!" without giving any clues as to what would be required to actually attend that school. Is it any wonder that students felt overwhelmed? The goal has been set, with no instructions as to how to achieve it.

Why go to college? Maybe a better question is, "What do you want to do for the rest of your life?" Education, career choices, and future earnings are all related to this decision. In 1997, President Clinton referred to education as "the fault line between those who will prosper in the new economy and those who will not" (¶ 1). His words are truer today than ever before.

Consider the following statistics from the U.S. Department of Education (2004):

- A high school dropout earned $22,100 per year in 2001.
- A high school graduate earned $30,056.
- A college graduate earned $54,704.
- In 1998, the male college graduate, aged 25 to 34, earned 63% more than his counterpart who did not attend college.

According to the 2001 U.S. Census, college graduates earned $1 million more during their lifetimes than high school graduates. Looking at this another way, the lifetime earnings of a person with a college degree is about three times that of a person without this education, or $1.5 million versus $500,000 (U.S. Census Bureau, 2004).

A recent research study (Barrow & Rouse, 2005) echoed the above results. Researchers estimated that the average cost of earning a 4-year college degree is about $107,277, which includes the average cost of tuition (about $30,000 for 4 years), plus the salary these young people would have earned if they had gone to work right out of high school.

Using the latest data, they estimated that a college degree would boost the total lifetime earnings of a student who entered school in 2003 by $402,959 over what they would have earned if they skipped college. That means the net value of a degree to the average student is roughly $295,682. A typical college graduate can expect to recoup his or her investment within 10 years.

We all have heard about people who became highly successful without a college education, but they are in the minority. We know who they are because their unusual achievement stands out. People without an education and job-related skills have a more difficult time finding work because they are competing against those who have more training. Further, if parents do not have a college education, the chances are that their children also will not attend college, primarily because their children never receive practical advice on applying to and attending college (Plank & Jordan, 2001). The reverse is also true: If you went to college, your children are more than twice as likely to attend.

Roughly two out of three young Americans do not go on to any form of higher education, and many of those who do enroll in postsecondary education don't end up graduating (Rowe, 2005). Almost half of those who never enrolled or dropped out said college wasn't for them because they wanted to work and make money. Almost as many said they couldn't afford college. Yet, by age 33, according to the College Board, the typical college graduate has earned enough to compensate for the cost of attending a 4-year public college or university, and has made up for his earnings passed up during his college years (Baum & Payea, 2004).

Some benefits of a college education are subtle, but real. The acquisition of knowledge is a very personal thing. People who go to college use the knowledge they acquire for the rest of their lives, and will continue to expand their knowledge and skills, express their thoughts more clearly in speech and in writing, grasp abstract concepts and theories, and increase their understanding of the world and community. College is likely to promote a love of learning in people as a result of developing new interests and passions.

3

Until people go away to college, their friends are acquired largely by circumstance from among their neighbors, the children they associate with in the first 12 grades of school, athletics teammates, religious education classmates, and other settings. Going away to college exposes an individual to a diverse group of people—some good, some not so good—and at a minimum, it provides more options from which to choose. The world is a rich place, full of places and experiences that can hardly be imagined by a person who never leaves his or her hometown. College exposes us to people from different national, ethnic, and religious groups, to different social and political ideas, to different income levels or ways of life, and even different ways of learning or absorbing information. A college education gives us courage to try new things, fosters our imagination to create new things, and gives us the freedom to think critically about everything we will ever see or hear in our lifetimes.

There are more than 3,500 colleges and universities in the United States. Choosing from among them is a complex task. Some students, particularly those who are gifted, are concerned about college and begin planning for it as early as elementary school. That being said, there are still many high school students who approach college planning and selection with less thought than they give to purchasing a video game or a new item of clothing. Lacking a plan, they may make arbitrary decisions based on inadequate information culled from a Web site, friend, or relative, simply because they do not know how to define the personal criteria needed to make college and career decisions. Far too many teenagers are simply not aware of how colleges differ, or how they can match their individual needs, wants, and desires with what a particular college may have to offer.

For many high school students, college planning is a finite process that begins and ends arbitrarily and abruptly. This process typically begins with participation in the Preliminary SAT®/National Merit Scholarship Qualifying Test (PSAT/NMSQT) during 11th grade, and ends with the receipt of acceptance or rejection letters from the schools to which the student applied. Between the two milestones—the

PSAT and letters of acceptance—students must select colleges they want to attend, complete a number of standardized achievement tests, and submit their applications. For many, the information they gather during the 11th and 12th grade is deemed sufficient to make decisions. For gifted students, however, a much longer process is necessary.

Gifted students should be concerned about and begin planning for college as early as the seventh grade, although many think about it earlier. They tend to make short mental lists that swing from one extreme to another: from "brand name" colleges, such as Harvard, Yale, Princeton, and Stanford, to popular state or community institutions. Their angst increases with each school year, building toward an event such as taking the PSAT, SAT, or ACT test. For gifted students, college planning should be one step in a life development process that takes place between 7th and 12th grade. This process begins with your child's self-awareness and ends with matching his or her needs with college offerings. Between those two points, you can expect your child to acquire many new skills and experiences, and grow with each activity. As your child grows in experience and self-awareness, he will be increasingly able to plan his future based on his talents, skills, interests, needs, values, and passions.

This guide is for parents and adolescents in the midst of the complex process of college and career planning. Parents, much of the book will speak to your concerns as you work with your child, but some sections are meant to be used by your child, and are therefore addressed to the student. Throughout the book you will find charts and checklists that will help you and your teen gradually come closer to selecting a list of appropriate colleges. While you and your child go through some of the exercises in the book, there are several things to keep in mind:

- There is no such thing as the perfect school. The college experience, like life, is a series of trade-offs. Most students should be able to identify several different types of schools appropriate for them. This does not mean that they would have identical experiences at each school, only that their experiences would be equally positive.

5

- The path from point A, knowing oneself, to point B, a satisfying college experience, does not necessarily follow a smooth progression. Adolescents develop intellectually, socially, and emotionally at inconsistent rates. They face the challenge of making a critical decision on college selection at a point in their lives when they have not finished "becoming themselves." Parents, teachers, and counselors should encourage students to think of college selection as the first step in what may ultimately be a multistep process. For example, the college environment suitable for a student's freshman and sophomore years may be unacceptable for the final 2 years, because the student—not the college—has changed. In such a case, transferring to another college is a realistic and positive option. This is an important point for the student who wants to attend a highly selective school, but does not have the qualifications to do so. A year at a less selective school may be followed by a transfer to the original school of choice if the student uses that year to prove he or she is capable of working at a challenging level.
- The most selective colleges receive more than 10 applications for every freshman vacancy. A large percentage of these applicants are highly qualified. If your adolescent aspires to a highly selective college, you can expect a highly competitive application review. Because your student's credentials will be examined so carefully and critically, knowing what he or she is up against before you begin can help make the college search more realistic.

Many college planning guides provide slick marketing tips for college applicants. But, unless the match between your child's needs and interests and the school's offering is truly a good one—and there is no way of knowing that without going through the kinds of activities proposed in this guide—students may be disappointed.

Students who can ask and begin to answer questions about themselves are on the road to developing self-awareness. When they can begin to ask and answer questions about colleges and relate those answers to themselves, they are prepared to begin the college selection process. Students *discover* themselves—that is, they identify personal values, aptitudes, and needs—and they learn how to conduct a college search through a multistep process. Ideally, this process should begin by seventh grade, with specific events occurring each subsequent year. However, the process can be shortened; it is never too late to begin. Included at the end of this chapter is a timeline to help your child throughout the college planning process.

Parents Providing Support and Encouragement

College planning and ultimately the transition to college are life-changing events for most teens, but keep in mind that all teens will have different reactions to the process. Some start making lists of potential colleges in the 7th grade, while others have not yet made plans for college at the start of 12th grade. One type of student may post rejection letters on a bedroom bulletin board, another may let the process affect her self-esteem, and a third student may take it in stride. Selecting a college is one of the first adult choices in life. There are no perfect solutions or clear-cut alternatives. It's an event that signals a transition to adulthood. Parents are often confused about how much guidance they can and should provide. You may teeter between withdrawal and taking over the process, not knowing how to strike a balance. You have an important role—becoming an informed consumer, and setting clear and realistic goals that reduce the pressure and keep things in perspective. You should support, encourage, and even empathize with your teenager, remembering your own experiences as a young adult. When you take time to learn about college planning and how it differs from your experience or that of someone you know, you can truly make a positive difference. As one student told her parents, "the best thing you did was to laugh at my jokes." She

7

was talking about having perspective, or college planning without any angst.

Some things for parents to keep in mind include the following:

- Getting into a brand-name school does not improve one's life. Teaching and learning are often better in schools you've never heard of.
- Be a guide on the side, gently encouraging your child, rather than an all-knowing sage on the stage. Be ready and able to demonstrate an understanding of the pressures these students are experiencing. Provide support.
- Know the critical skills your child needs to make major decisions.
- Understand how he or she defines the important characteristics of his or her ideal college.
- Help your child find specific institutions that meet his or her individual needs.
- Set clear and realistic goals that reduce the pressure on your child and keep things in perspective.
- Think of yourself as a shepherd. Your job is to guide and protect. Some parents avoid interfering by withdrawing. Some parents are overbearing. Neither extreme is useful.
- Discuss college openly, gearing conversation toward what your son or daughter needs from a college and why—city or country environment, emphasis on Greek life, sports, student/faculty ratio, class size, special programs, etc.
- Listen to your youngster. Pay particular attention to what attracts him or her to certain schools.
- *Do not* type applications, correct essays, or call colleges for information for your child. When a student has questions, an admissions office would prefer to hear from the student.
- *Do* keep track of dates such as those for standardized tests, admissions deadlines, financial aid deadlines, and so forth. Adolescents experience considerable pressure during their last 2 years in high school. Often, they need someone else to keep track of some of the details.
- *Do* make photocopies of all applications because it's almost inevitable that a big typo will crawl onto the page.

Proofread everything for errors, but do not make style or grammar changes. *Do not* edit your child's work. Be sure to make copies of completed applications.

- Discuss any limitations up front. Find out all you can about financial aid. If money is a problem, as it is for most people, discuss it rationally and explain that the family will need to take advantage of available scholarships, loans, or any other source of funds. But, don't restrict your child's choices based solely on cost, because some colleges provide financial aid to all of their students.
- The college planning process is part of a life development process in which there are *no* right answers. The process is different for every person because the goal is to make a match between your child's strengths and interests and college offerings. The college that is perfect for someone you know may be totally wrong for your child. Let your student make his or her final decisions and own the process.
- The college search is like an arranged marriage. Make the best match you can—love will come later.

College Planning Timeline, Grades 7-12

The search for the ideal college begins well before a student's senior year in high school. There are many things students must do prior to their senior year to lay the groundwork for the college search. The following timeline is approximately what students need to complete during the middle and high school years, and should be given to students for their personal use. It provides hints and tips on what your student can do to make sure he or she is on schedule.

9

Seventh Grade

- If your family hasn't started saving for college, start now.
- In the seventh and eighth grades, classes are divided into separate academic subjects. Take advantage of opportu-

nities to explore and investigate new academic areas and extracurricular activities.

- Take time to learn about yourself.
- Examine and evaluate academic options that may be available in your community. For example, is a high school magnet program available? Are school enrichment programs offered in your community? Looking ahead, does your community offer schools with an Advanced Placement (AP) or International Baccalaureate (IB) program? If you hope to attend a high school with a challenging academic program, plan now. Investigate all of these avenues.
- If you think you might benefit from an accelerated program, there are several ways to accomplish this, including sources of enrichment such as regional talent search programs, university-based summer programs, internships, mentorships, and working toward college credit in high school.
- Many seventh-grade students take the SAT or the ACT assessment test between seventh and eighth grade in order to become eligible for talent search programs, as well as other opportunities. Ask your guidance counselor how you can participate in a regional talent search process by taking the SAT, ACT, or another nationally normed test. Some talent search programs will accept a standardized test used by your school. Students who require extended time, fee waivers, or an alternative day of the week because of religious reasons should contact talent search programs early in September.
- Many summer programs offer a variety of opportunities for you to explore interests, try new academic courses, refine skills, make friends, and live away from home. Summer programs vary in quality, so investigate them carefully. If the price of a program prevents you from participating, find out whether scholarships are available from the program or from local sources. Some summer programs offer partial scholarships to match local gifts.
- If you are ready, seek opportunities to obtain high school credit, particularly in foreign languages and mathematics.

- Begin to think objectively and realistically about your abilities, aptitudes, values, and interests, and how you learn best. Begin to think about your aspirations and goals.
- Seek ways to expand your horizons. Take risks and try new courses and activities. Some high-school-level courses you take now may appear on your high school transcript. However, the grades you earn in middle school classes will be far less important to colleges than the grades you earn in high school.
- Investigate ways to study efficiently and manage your time. You will find a learning strategies database online (see http://www.muskingum.edu/home/cal) that can help.
- Read a wide variety of materials, including books, newspapers, and magazines.
- Practice your writing skills. Keep a journal. Write short stories, poetry, and prose, and enter contests. Are you working on a mathematics or science project? Record your impressions and prepare a story about your work. Submit your work to your school newspaper and other publications.
- Look for opportunities to do volunteer work.

Eighth Grade

- During this year, discuss the transition to high school with your parents and guidance counselor. Develop a master plan that includes an academic plan listing courses required for high school graduation and courses you *want* to take during the next 4 years. Select courses that are as challenging as you think you can handle.
- Many people have trouble managing time. There is always more that we want to do and less time to do it. When you draft your 4-year plan, try to create a time management plan that will address the hours you spend in classes, the hours needed for homework, and the time you want for extracurricular interests, family activities, rest, and relaxation. Keep your time management plan flexible and creative, not overstructured. You can review it once in a while to see if it needs adjustment.

- Look for ways to investigate career options and opportunities. Talk to family and friends about what they do at work from the time they arrive, to the time they leave. Although seventh or eighth grade is much too early to make college and career decisions, you can learn something to use later on.
- Volunteer your time. This is an excellent way to explore careers and develop community spirit.
- Look for ways to strengthen your study skills in specific academic areas. Improving study skills can help you manage your time wisely.
- Plan a creative summer. Many programs have early enrollment deadlines. Start planning no later than December.

Ninth Grade

- By ninth grade, you should have drafted a 4-year plan that will help you decide the courses you need, and how you can use your in-school and afterschool hours most effectively. Build a flexible schedule that will accommodate time for studying, extracurricular activities, exercise, and relaxing.
- Find out about the extracurricular activities you would like to become involved in. Look for activities that include community service or leadership opportunities. Share your talents with others by volunteering. Helping others is a great way to learn something about yourself. Pursue any hobbies or sports that interest you. Get involved.
- Register for the PSAT and take it for practice. Obtain a free Student Bulletin (visit http://www.collegeboard.com) to learn what the test is like, how students may prepare, and how scores are reported and used. Make sure you are practicing with the latest version of the test.
- The more selective colleges will check to see whether or not your courses represent the most challenging program offered by your high school. If you want challenging courses in 11th and 12th grade, you need to take the prerequisites. Think about the following:

- ○ What courses are required for high school graduation?
- ○ How many years of each subject are required for college admission?
- ○ What additional academic areas would you like to explore that are not offered by your high school (e.g., philosophy, archaeology)? Consider a summer program.
- ○ What extracurricular activities do you want to fit into your schedule?
- ○ What activities are you committed to that you want to continue?
- ○ What activities do you want to eliminate?
- ○ What portion of college costs will be your responsibility? Do you need to work during high school?

- If your high school includes a career center or multimedia center, get to know the people who work there and the resources available. Explore computer-assisted college planning programs.
- Read widely. Exposure to different kinds of material will improve your vocabulary and language skills. Read newspapers (your local paper, *The New York Times*, *USA Today*, and others), magazines (news, business, sports, and special interest magazines), and books (biography, history, science fiction, adventure, novels, poetry, and drama).
- In the spring, review your 4-year plan with your guidance counselor and parents and decide if you can handle highly challenging courses the following year.

Tenth Grade

- The PSAT/NMSQT is given in October. Be sure to sign up. In 11th grade, your PSAT scores are used to determine your eligibility for the National Merit Scholarship and the National Merit Hispanic Scholarship. Scores don't count this year—just take the PSAT for practice. See your guidance counselor for instructions on how to sign up.

13

- Through the PSAT, you may get mail from colleges and universities that are interested in students like you. Start a filing system to organize the information you receive. A couple of oversized shoe boxes may work for now, but later you will want something that is easier to use, such as file folders.
- Become familiar with college reference books published by the College Board, Peterson's, Fiske, and other organizations. Visiting a local library or bookstore will help you get to know different types of reference materials and what each can do for you.
- Visit a nearby college and take a tour. Check to see whether your school has college videos.
- Take SAT Subject Tests at the end of 10th grade in any subjects in which you have done well but do not plan to continue studying in high school (e.g., biology, foreign language). Most students take the subject tests toward the end of their junior year or at the beginning of their senior year, but you should take tests in subjects such as world history, biology, chemistry, or physics as soon as possible after completing the corresponding courses, while the material is still fresh in your mind. For foreign language tests, you'll do better after at least 2 years of study.
- Plan a meaningful summer activity. Consider an internship, volunteer work, travel, or spending time with someone who works in a career that interests you.
- Get more involved in your favorite extracurricular activity. Look for leadership opportunities. Colleges look for *depth* of involvement.
- Continue reading a wide variety of materials. The more you read, the broader your vocabulary will expand.
- Look into careers. Investigate computer-assisted career guidance programs such as Career Occupational Preference System (COPS; http://www.edits.net/cops.html), Career Options (http://www.rileyguide.com/careers.html), SIGI[3] (http://www.valparint.com), or DISCOVER (http://www.act.org/discover). If your school doesn't have them, ask the nearest community college career center.

- Find out whether or not your high school administers vocational aptitude tests, interest inventories, learning style inventories, or personality tests. Take all available assessment tests and make an appointment with your counselor to discuss the results.
- Become familiar with the *O*net Dictionary of Occupational Titles* and the *Occupational Outlook Handbook* (see pp. 82–84 for more information on these and other resources). Pick one or two careers and read about them. Spend some time with someone who works in those fields.
- By the end of 10th grade, review your 4-year plan and high school transcript with your guidance counselor and parents. Plan for 11th grade by signing up for challenging academic courses, but leave time for rest, relaxation, family activities, your favorite extracurricular activities, and community service.

Eleventh Grade

- Discuss college plans with your parents and counselor. Your parents should make an appointment with your counselor to facilitate these discussions. Family discussions with a student's counselor early in the year help clarify everyone's expectations.
- Begin the college search process. Attend College Night at your school and go to an area college fair. Speak with college representatives when they visit your school, even if you think you are not interested in the school they represent. Compare and contrast what they tell you, what you have read, and what you have seen for yourself.
- Sign up for the October PSAT. This time the scores count! Obtain a Student Bulletin (free from the College Board) to learn what the test is like, how you may prepare, and how your scores are reported and used. (See http://www.collegeboard.com for more information.)
- Make sure you are familiar with the most recent changes to the SAT or the ACT. Ask your target schools which test they prefer and plan to take one or the other in the spring.

15

- If your scores are not as high as you expected, consider taking a prep course. Remember, the cost of a course may not reflect its quality. Try to find one in which the instructor will analyze your answer sheet, provide you with specific information on your strengths and weaknesses, and offer tips and hints on how to raise your scores. There are Web sites that will do this too, such as Barnes & Noble's Sparknotes (http://www.sparknotes.com).
- Take SAT Subject Tests in subjects you will complete at the end of this school year or in courses such as a foreign language, even if you plan to continue taking the courses in further depth.
- If you are taking AP courses and doing extremely well, consider taking AP tests. Choose carefully: Some colleges offer exemption, credit, or both for AP grades of 3, 4, or 5. If you take AP tests someplace other than your school, be sure your grades are reported to your high school and sent to the college of your choice.
- Discuss finances with your family. Plan now for summer or part-time jobs if your family expects you to pay for part of your education. Begin early.
- Keep up a good level of academic achievement. This is the year that really counts. Balance work, play, and extracurricular activities. Colleges like to see an upward trend in your grade point average.
- Request financial aid bulletins from all of your target schools. Go online to get the Free Application for Federal Student Aid (FAFSA) and take your family through the process of completing one (http://www.fafsa.ed.gov).
- If you want to play sports for a National Collegiate Athletic Association (NCAA) Division I or II team, register with the NCAA Clearinghouse (1-800-638-3731, or go to http://www.ncaa.org) before the end of your junior year.
- By the end of 11th grade, review your 4-year plan and high school transcript with your parents and guidance counselor. Are you satisfied with your progress? Are you accomplishing your goals?

Twelfth Grade

- Review your list of colleges. You should have a file on each college you are considering.
- Review admissions criteria for the schools that interest you. Send for applications.
- Many colleges use data from CSS/Financial Aid PRO-FILE® to provide nonfederal financial aid. Begin applying online at https://profileonline.collegeboard.com.
- Begin the scholarship search. Check out http://www.fastweb.com and http://www.finaid.org. Complete and mail the FAFSA or submit it electronically after January 1.
- Identify at least two teachers and two other people who know you well who could write solid recommendations for you. If you are applying for early admission or early decision, line up recommendations as soon as possible. Make appointments to see them to review your accomplishments and goals. Follow up. It is *your* responsibility to make sure that letters of recommendation arrive before the colleges' deadlines.
- Sign up to retake the SAT or ACT if you think you can raise your scores. Make sure that your SAT or ACT scores are sent to your guidance counselor and the schools to which you are applying. Review your scores with your guidance counselor and ask for an interpretation that relates to the schools you are considering.
- Check out http://www.commonapp.org to see which colleges accept the common application, and fill it out if necessary.
- Find out when your high school registrar or guidance counselor sends your applications, transcripts, letters of recommendation, and supporting materials to the colleges. Early in December is typical, but some high schools set earlier deadlines. Early decision deadlines are usually in November. If your school does not send application forms and supporting material to the colleges for you, then *you* must be sure to send everything *on time*. Pay attention to deadlines.

17

- Photocopy *everything* before sending the application packages to colleges.
- Carefully review your high school transcript. If some courses listed are not easy to identify, be sure to add a description of those courses. An example is an honors course that doesn't say "honors" in the course name. Also, be sure your school profile or transcript supplement is included, especially if you are applying out of state, where admissions staff might not be familiar with your high school.
- Maintain or continue to improve your academic standing. Most colleges look unfavorably upon an applicant whose grades are falling. Schools will revoke admission for students whose grades have slipped. If one of your grades is falling, you may want to write a letter of explanation.
- Visit the colleges you are seriously considering.
- Update your college planning portfolio. Be sure to add recent achievements and new events that have occurred.
- If you haven't received any financial aid packages by April, call the colleges to make sure the necessary information arrived. Send the acceptance notice and a deposit to the college you have chosen. Shop for school supplies!

Planning for Gifted Students: What Makes Them Different?

sabel is able to read maps quickly, can plan routes, and is often nominated as the trip planner when her family and friends travel. In preparation for a college interview 300 miles away, she analyzed six different routes to find the most direct and scenic route. When the family reached their destination, Isabel was greeted by the interviewer, who casually asked, "How was your trip?" Isabel spent the half-hour interview explaining the six alternative routes and the reasons for her choice, missing an opportunity to ask for information that was not mentioned in the catalog and other material, as well as an opportunity to explain how and why she would be a good match for that college. If Isabel had practiced the college interview and understood its purpose, she might have been able to make the most of her interview opportunity.

In high school, Alex was fascinated by the relationship among the ideas of Einstein, Picasso, and James Joyce. He developed a paper, entitled "The Climate of Opinion in the Early 20th Century," relating Einstein's theory of relativity, Picasso's cubist work, and Joyce's *A Portrait of the*

Artist as a Young Man. Alex's thesis was that a fragmentation of reality had occurred simultaneously in mathematics, art, and literature. Alex's social studies teacher noted that the paper was late and reduced his grade from A to B. The teacher also noted Alex's problem with deadlines in the college recommendations he prepared. Other teachers noted that Alex sometimes did not complete assignments at all. Because all of the work he completed was superb, his grades were usually B's and C's, which equaled a balance among the A's for what had been completed on time, the B's for late work, and the F's for assignments that were never turned in. Alex had a problem. He needed a college like St. John's College (whose two campuses are located in Annapolis, MD, and Santa Fe, NM) that would nurture his talents and passion for abstract conceptualization. But, how was he going to find such a school, and how was he going to get in?

Jack wrote award-winning poetry and created sensitive lyrics for musical productions. When his class graduated from high school, he wrote a commemorative limerick. The title, "O Pioneers!" paraphrased Willa Cather. Jack referred to his classmates' 4 years together as a "differential calculus" of experiences. Jack's English teacher constantly criticized Jack's elaborate creative compositions, focusing primarily on the structure of the language used, punctuation, and rules of grammar. Jack received C's and D's because he did not follow the teacher's specific grammatical model. He frequently was unable to produce what was expected; therefore, his grade point average was not spectacular. Jack was extremely gifted and needed to attend a school where his talents would be appreciated and developed, such as Grinnell College in Iowa or Middlebury College in Vermont, both small liberal arts schools. However, with his grade point average, he had to communicate clear goals and actively persuade a college that he was capable of college-level work.

The above vignettes describe students who are gifted and quite different from one another, although they share some common experiences. They were not necessarily recognized or identified as gifted, but they have some of the characteristics of gifted students that affect their college planning. Two of these traits are multipotentiality (multiple talents) and sensitivity to competing expectations. Other special populations of gifted students we'll discuss include students who are learning disabled, homeschooled students, and underachieving gifted students.

Multipotential Gifted Students

Keesha is a multipotential gifted student. As a high school junior, she had boundless enthusiasm for everything and an endless supply of energy. Her interests included psychology, creative writing, language, physics, chemistry, jewelry making, dancing, swimming, being outdoors, science fiction, and "people." The lead cross country runner in her grade, she was also in the top 10% of her grade and had already taken AP English. Keesha had a strong desire to be of service to humanity, and she wanted to master 12 languages before she turned 40.

If the above vignette sounds like your gifted student, you may be anxiously looking forward to the day she will get a driver's license, and be able to drive to all of her activities alone. Gifted students are highly capable and many participate in a variety of activities. Often, their calendars present an intimidating display of appointment dates and times. Many multitalented students have heard the saying, "You can be anything you want," over and over again. But, that is precisely the problem. They seem to suffer from a wealth of

21

abilities. Some of these youngsters excel in every academic subject and activity. Keesha wonders how she will be able to make college and career plans when, on the surface, she likes everything and is good at everything. Students like her experience vocational selection as an existential dilemma. They are as concerned about the road not taken as they are with finding the right path. For Keesha, choosing to be a linguist means giving up a career as a physicist. Many underchallenged secondary students fill up their lives with many activities, either to avoid boredom or because they think they need to appear to be well-rounded for future college applications. If this attitude is carried over into the college setting, the attempt to participate in everything may create a destructive academic and emotional environment for Keesha. It would be much better if she would choose a few activities and focus on them, eventually assuming a leadership role.

Vocational exploration and aptitude tests, intended to provide guidance by showing students their areas of strength and matching those strengths to careers, are of little use to students like Keesha, because these tests showed evenly high aptitudes, abilities, and interests in every area. One young student, upon receiving his vocational aptitude scores, said, "I can be a nuclear physicist or a plumber. How do I choose?"

Sensitivity to Expectations

Marcus is the middle child of three. His parents expected that all of their children would excel in school, and indeed his older and younger sisters were always on the honor roll and succeeded in everything they did. In school, Marcus was more interested in making friends than in earning grades, and when his grades began to drop in eighth grade, his parents sent him to a private school that instilled in him a solid respect for achievement. Marcus attended an Ivy League college, followed by law school. He passed the bar with flying colors and opened a law office. But, something wasn't right; Marcus was unhappy. So, one day he closed his practice and went to Hollywood to become an actor. Marcus was highly sensitive to expectations. His parents never had to say anything because he knew that high achievement and a profession were expected. But, he had a passion for acting, one that had never been fulfilled. Fortunately, he was young enough to change careers and realized that law was never going to provide the inner satisfaction he needed.

Sensitivity and receptivity are great assets, and they permit a student to be receptive to imaginative, creative ideas. Like multipotentiality, however, these characteristics can be a mixed blessing when students plan for college and a career. Parents, relatives, friends, siblings, teachers, and coaches—all with the best of intentions—are eager to add their own expectations and observations to the bright student's intentions and goals. The dilemma is complicated by the numerous options within the reach of a highly talented student.

Heightened sensitivity is often accompanied by heightened vulnerability to criticism, suggestions, and emotional appeals from others. Often, others' expectations for talented young people compete with the pull of their own dreams and plans. Some youngsters do not even think about what they want. They become so conflicted by all the advice they receive that they postpone going to college or attend college and change their major several times, prolonging their graduation.

Gifted Students With Disabilities

23

Over the past decade, clinicians and practitioners have devoted extraordinary time and energy to providing parents and teachers with clues for identifying children with learning disabilities and other disabilities. Parents, however, often sense that their child is somehow different long before they receive confirmation from a consulting psychologist or the school.

Disabilities can affect gifted students in many areas, whether it is difficulty paying attention or staying on task, or specific identified learning disabilities, such as dyslexia. At home or at school your child may be oblivious to time; may appear to be lazy, forgetful, or unprepared; or may honestly believe that a project or chore has been completed when it has hardly begun. She may have trouble concentrating on completing rote assignments or classroom lectures, but can spend hours engaged in research on a topic of her interest. He may have difficulties reading and comprehending material and need assistive technology, such as books on tape, to get him through long reading assignments.

But, what happens if your child has disabilities and is gifted? Gifted students with learning disabilities (often called twice-exceptional) have much in common with other gifted students. They typically have an excellent long-term memory, an extensive vocabulary, and they grasp abstract concepts and thrive on complexity. They are highly creative, imaginative, perceptive, and insightful, and they are keen observers. They also have much in common with other students who have learning disabilities, such as a poor short-term memory and poor organizational skills. Their handwriting is frequently illegible, they struggle with easy, sequential material, and rote memorization is almost impossible. They may be unable to learn unless they are interested in the topic. These students perform poorly on timed tests. Yet, only a small percentage of gifted students with learning disabilities are identified, in part because they use their giftedness in ways that compensate for their limitations. Thus, the giftedness masks the learning disability, and the disability masks the giftedness, so that neither is visible in the classroom.

Giftedness may combine with almost any area of disability, with the possible exception of disabilities that are accompanied by mental retardation. Each combination is unique, but many twice-exceptional people are highly accomplished. For example, take Matt Savage, an autistic child who is an internationally known jazz pianist. Matt was awarded the American Society of Composers, Authors and Publishers (ASCAP) Young Jazz Composer award in 2005 (see http://www.savagerecords.com). Children with Williams Syndrome (see http://www.williams-syndrome.org), a rare genetic condition that causes medical and developmental problems, may be superbly musical, and despite their difficulties, many are professional musicians. Children with Asperger's Syndrome seem to soak up knowledge and develop expertise in areas of interest; however, they have severe problems with social skills. Children with dyslexia often have a high level of spatial intelligence (West, 1997). Children with Attention Deficit/Hyperactivity Disorder (ADHD) have many talents and strengths. They may be able to do double-digit subtraction in their heads, but can't concentrate long enough to learn things that most children find simple.

For gifted children with disabilities, the more difficult and complex tasks may be the easiest; however, simple tasks may be beyond their capabilities. Some are placed in gifted programs where their low grades are chalked up to laziness or bad attitude. Others languish in special education classes where they are literally bored to tears by drill-and-kill math exercises and too-simple reading primers. Then, there are those students whose gifts and disabilities are so evenly balanced that they are presumed to be average and left to fend for themselves in mainstream classes (Baum, 1990).

The following case study and discussion of the college and career planning process makes clear how infinitely more complex that process may be when the gifted adolescent has significant learning disabilities.

When he was an infant, a major university hospital identified Anthony's brain abnormalities as resulting from birth trauma. His parents were told they were lucky his troubles were identified so early in his life. During his early childhood, different medical professionals diagnosed Anthony's problems as a variety of disorders, including mental retardation, brain damage, dyslexia, minimal brain dysfunction,

25

and learning disabilities. His IQ scores varied from below average to above average, depending on which person evaluated him. Recommendations for Anthony's schooling ranged from placement in a therapeutic day nursery, to a special education facility, to a mainstream environment. His parents were told a gamut of things, including that he either needed a self-contained class, a resource class, or no special arrangements at all.

One expert said Anthony was perfectly normal, suffering only from overanxious parents. Others blamed his problems on assorted psychological experiences, none related to birth trauma or learning disability. Anthony progressed through the expected developmental stages, but always at his own unique pace. He walked with difficulty, and at age 3, he could barely talk. In nursery school he made progress in gross motor skills and reading readiness. His fine motor skills were very poor, and his socialization skills were nonexistent.

At age 5, Anthony began to read, developed a rich vocabulary, made insightful, though garbled, comments, and accelerated rapidly in reading skills. Preschool teachers missed the signs of his giftedness, focusing instead on toilet habits and his inability to write his name legibly. A private school specializing in children with learning disabilities proved inappropriate. At home he read every book given to him, but the school proudly reported that he had mastered "three new letters this quarter." The school admitted it was impeding his academic progress.

When he was ready for elementary school, Anthony asked to enter public school. He knew he had difficulties and worked harder than his peers to achieve modest results. Despite hours of assistance, he could not remember recently learned facts and had difficulty following simple directions. Arithmetic proved almost insurmountable. He felt academically superior in self-contained classrooms but could not cope with impersonal regular classes. Socialization remained a problem.

By high school, his reading level was excellent, and his understanding of content was accurate and compassionate. He developed a keen interest in computers. His speech was still difficult to understand, his memory was spotty, and he could not learn arithmetic or write a coherent sentence. The school's protocol for planning an academic program allowed maximum mainstreaming and capitalized on Anthony's strengths and wishes. His preferences led to family negotiations about subjects he needed or were important, or where he would do well, might fail, or need help. He took courses no special education student had taken (e.g., 3 years of foreign language and 2 years of computer science). He refused, over the school's objection, to take traditional special education courses. Despite this approach, some teachers resisted his presence, and others placed meaningless burdens on him.

By his senior year, it was clear that Anthony had an exceptional mind for specific areas of study. His reading and vocabulary abilities were significantly above grade level, he had a knack for computer science, and he developed a strong interest in and understanding of politics. He still could not do arithmetic, spell, or write legibly, but he finished high school with a fine record and was elected to the National Honor Society. He certainly had learning disabilities, but clearly demonstrated traits and characteristics associated with giftedness.

After an extensive search for colleges with support programs, one was identified that met all the criteria that had been set. He took courses offered to the entire student body, but received tutorial support in all subject areas. By his junior year, he had made the Dean's List and was elected into a national scholastic honor society. Anthony graduated and went on to earn a master's degree in experimental psychology, challenged again by a professor more focused on legibility than content. Now, Anthony holds a professional computer technology position with the federal government, is married, owns his own home, and is the father of a baby boy.

Special Concerns

The decision to send a child with learning disabilities to college (regardless of his or her giftedness) is not one to be taken lightly. For an individual with deficits in social, study, and organizational skills, it is a major decision. Support systems meticulously worked out in high school cannot follow the student to college. Parent advocacy must be replaced by self-advocacy. Academic learning must be pursued while a medley of independent living skills is developed, friends are sought, and separation from home and family is realized. The learning-disabled student who is thinking of attending college must be made aware of all these difficulties and understand that the choice to attend or not to attend is his or her own decision to make.

Once your gifted and learning-disabled child realizes he is capable of attending a college, the personal (Who am I?) and college (Who are they and what will they expect of me?) evaluations should begin. Discussions also should begin with guidance counselors and college advisers. Just like with any other college-bound student, there are college fairs to attend, guides and directories to review, visits to be made, and applications to be completed.

Like all gifted students, your child needs to understand her own abilities and limitations, and guide her own transition planning by looking at various postsecondary options. For a student with learning disabilities, the basic college planning steps and schedules are similar in many ways to those for a more typical student. Your child needs to become familiar with how he learns best. Many successful students with learning disabilities acquire compensatory learning strategies to help them use the knowledge they have accumulated, to plan, complete, and evaluate projects, and to take an active role in shaping their environments. Your child needs to learn how to apply learning strategies flexibly, and how to modify or create strategies fluently to fit new learning situations. For example, compensatory strategies may include:

- allowing more time to complete tests, papers, and other projects;
- listening to audio tapes of textbooks while reading; and
- making up words to remind your child to use his or her prior knowledge.

You and your learning-disabled child must expand upon the basics of college planning and focus on specific, unique issues. For example:

- You must learn to distinguish between schools that merely accept students with learning disabilities as a condition of continuing federal support from those that actively encourage the enrollment of these students by providing specialized programs for them.
- You must investigate the school's support to determine whether it is unstructured (provided as needed) or structured (records on the student are maintained and progress is monitored).

As the list of college criteria is assembled, you and your child must be honest about your perceptions of his or her needs. Basic questions, such as the school's distance from home and available transportation for home visits, single-sex education or coeducation, the size of the student body, and academic standing, must be expanded to include issues such as the following:

- Is there evidence of an organized program to aid students with learning disabilities?

29

- Is there evidence of a full-time staff in the program, as well as a full-time director to monitor activities?
- Is there evidence of special considerations for learning-disabled students, such as allowing tape recorders in the classroom, untimed tests, writing laboratories, tutors in every subject area, and allowance of extended time for graduation?
- Is there evidence of successful career placements of students in their chosen fields following graduation?

As with any college search, your child's list will narrow to between five and seven good candidate schools. The schools must then be contacted, interviews arranged, and family visits planned. Campus tours and the opportunity to sit in on classes must be given particular attention, because it is extremely important for your child to personally judge the level of difficulty of the instruction, observe the interaction of other students, and gain for himself a sense of the relationship between the students and the faculty.

The admissions interview may not answer all the questions regarding programs designed for gifted students with learning disabilities. If this is so, you and your child must seek out and meet with a member of the learning disabilities program staff. A list of questions based on family concerns and perhaps stimulated by a review of the college directories and guides or discussions with high school guidance personnel should be prepared prior to the visit. Questions might include the following:

- What type of support is available for students with disabilities?
- Does a full-time professional staff monitor the program?
- Has the program been evaluated, and if so, by whom?
- Are there any concerns for the program's future?
- Who counsels students during registration, orientation, and course selection?
- For which courses is tutoring available?
- What kind of tutoring is available, and who does it—peers or staff?

- Is tutoring automatically provided, or must the student request assistance?
- How well do faculty members accept students with learning disabilities?
- May students take a lighter load each semester instead of the traditional 12–15 hours?
- Are courses in study skills or writing skills offered?
- Have counselors who work with these students received special training?
- How do students on campus spend their free time? Are there programs that will interest and accommodate them?
- May students take more time to graduate?
- Who can parents contact if they have concerns during the academic year?
- Is assistive technology available or permitted in the classroom? (Word processors with text-to-speech software, outlining, word prediction, and speech recognition capabilities offer assistive capabilities depending on a person's specific disabilities.)

The adolescent's progress toward adulthood is constantly stymied by dilemma. The dilemma faced by students, most particularly the gifted student with disabilities, stems from their desire to demonstrate independence from parents, counselors, teachers, and tutors, and the equally strong desire to maintain the respect and support of those same parents, counselors, teachers, and tutors. Students frequently wish to make the decisions that will frame their future, even while sensing that they may not be realistic or ultimately doable.

College and career planning for gifted students with disabilities is practical, but it requires extraordinary participation, cooperation, and patience.

Legal Issues

31

The 2004 update of the Individuals with Disabilities Education Act (IDEA; 1990) requires that the Individualized Education Program (IEP) team consider postschool goals when the student is about to enter high school at about age 14. Beginning at age 16 (or younger, if appropriate) a statement of transition services needed by the student must be included in the IEP. Once students with disabilities graduate from high school, they are no longer eligible for services provided by the school system, including an IEP. The Americans with Disabilities Act (ADA; 1990) bars discrimination against students with disabilities during the college admissions process. Once admitted, students may request reasonable accommodations to allow them to participate in courses, exams, and other activities. Most colleges and universities have a disability support services office to help provide accommodations.

The following suggestions may help those who guide gifted students with learning disabilities:

- Students must understand their strengths and learning needs not only to be successful in coursework, but also to identify and request the accommodations they will require.
- Colleges require documentation of a disability (i.e., results of tests indicating the presence of a disability) in order to provide support services; having an IEP or Section 504 plan in high school is not enough documentation to obtain services from colleges.
- Students should be informed that there are several forms of the SAT, ACT, and many other standardized tests. Students may request to take an untimed version of the SAT or the ACT, but arrangements must be made well in advance. For more information, check out the SAT Services for Students with Disabilities Web site at http://www.collegeboard.com/ssd/student. The ACT Services for Students with Disabilities Web site is http://www.act.org/aap/disab.
- Students who might have difficulty completing a written or typed college application should investigate a computerized method of completing a college application.

Homeschooled Students

Matt was a very bright child with a quick mind who mastered schoolwork easily. By the time he reached second grade, it was obvious to his parents that he was getting bored and the public school was no longer a match for Matt's abilities. At first, his parents were reluctant to homeschool Matt and his older brother, because neither parent had attended college. However, his parents did opt to homeschool the brothers, and when needed, the family readily sought outside help, especially in curricular areas where the parents had little expertise.

At age 12, Matt became the youngest student ever to enroll in the local junior college. The boys thrived in this environment and participated in Little League sports for many years. Matt's basketball team was made up of homeschooled students. Because the brothers were homeschooled and moved through the curricula at their own pace, the family had great flexibility and had time for many types of activities. Completion of a series of junior college classes enabled Matt to complete 18 hours of college courses before graduating from high school. Matt's mother kept a highly detailed transcript of his courses and activities. His first-choice school, Baylor University, a large private university, accepted Matt's application for enrollment.

Matt says that homeschooling gave him an independence that served him well in college. His advice to current high school students who are homeschooled? "Do not let the pace of your public school peers dictate to you the pace of your dreams. Don't wait until you're a college sophomore before you start identifying your gifts and dreams and setting goals toward achieving those dreams." Matt graduated from Baylor after 4 successful years, excelling academically, socially, and as a member of the university's Student Government. He now attends law school full-time.

Are you a homeschooling parent? If so, your children are part of the more than 1 million students in the U.S. who are homeschooled. If your adolescent is in high school, you may have wondered about the transition into college. If college admission is so competitive, how are you going to help your homeschooled teen stand out?

Keep a Journal

Parents who are homeschooling secondary students will find that keeping a journal is key to sanity, because it's almost impossible to recreate 4 to 6 years of school for a college application. The journal can be anything you want it to be, but some items are necessary, such as lists of courses taken and texts used, and examples of your child's work, such as essays, reading logs, sheets of math problems, and photographs of him doing lab work. If your teen needs advanced subjects in one or more academic areas where you don't have expertise, you have probably looked for someone with advanced skills and the interest to serve as a mentor. If possible, it would be helpful if that person also kept a journal, or some type of record that would document your child's path through high school.

Extracurricular or Outside Activities

If your child wishes to attend a competitive college or apply for scholarships, he or she should participate in extracurricular activities. Homeschoolers have a distinct advantage in this area. They may not have the resources of a traditional school, but they have the time to be involved in activities other than those offered at a traditional high school. For example, one homeschooled student who was interested in political science interned for a state delegate and lobbied on Capitol Hill. Other students have started their own magazine instead of working on the school paper. Others have gone on overseas missions trips. College-bound homeschoolers should use the extra time they have gained from individualized learning to gain real-world experiences that look good on college and scholarship applications.

Taking Tests

Many homeschooled students are concerned about taking tests, because they haven't had much practice. The SAT has undergone radical changes in the last few years, and it's a good idea to become familiar with the revised test, as well as the scoring quirks that accompany any complex test. On the Barnes & Noble Sparknotes Web site you can find an online book—*The New SAT*—that consists of 21 chapters that can be searched easily onscreen. It explains anything you would ever want to know about the SAT. The Web site also provides an essay grading service and three practice tests with diagnostic software that analyzes your results immediately and provides feedback on how to improve. For more information, visit http://www.sparknotes.com.

Statistics from the SAT and ACT college entrance exams (Rudner, 1999) indicate that homeschooled students do perform competitively compared to traditional students. In 1999, students who identified themselves as homeschooled scored an average of 1083 out of 1600 on the SAT, 67 points above the national average, and an average score of 22.7 on the ACT, compared with the national average of 21. Sixty-nine percent of homeschoolers go on to college, compared with 71% of public high schools graduates and 90% of private school graduates. How do they get in without transcripts? Parents put together portfolios with samples of their children's work and lists of their accomplishments. Transcripts are created at home, and standardized test scores are included in the portfolio.

One of the problems encountered by homeschooled students is the potential for fewer contacts with college admission representatives. College representatives typically visit high schools to provide information to students and look for student academic stars, musicians, athletes, and so forth. Students enrolled in high school can take advantage of the interaction with college staff by asking questions about the school, lifestyle, academic rating, and anything else that is important. Homeschooled students need to find other ways to interact with college staff from a wide range of postsecondary institutions. College fairs provide that opportunity. The National Association for College Admission Counseling (NACAC) Web site (http://www.nacacnet.org) offers a list of college fairs and their locations and dates.

Colleges now consider the use of portfolios, a transcript prepared by a parent, and SAT and ACT results as legitimate methods of assessing homeschooled students' preparation for college. More than two thirds of American colleges now accept parent-created transcripts, although some require homeschooled applicants to submit a GED or additional standardized test scores that provide admissions officers the necessary context for assessing students' abilities (NACAC, 2005). It's best if your adolescent asks the school he or she is interested in what it expects in terms of objective information (e.g., GPA, class rank, test scores). Homeschoolers now attend 900 colleges of all types. Harvard accepts approximately 10 homeschooled students every year. Some schools actively recruit homeschoolers, because they tend to be highly focused and goal oriented. Harvard University, Purdue University, and the University of Texas are all homeschooler-friendly and impart some good advice for anyone interested in attending the school.

Underachieving Students

Alicia (an identified gifted ninth-grade student) could not put her name on the paper. She was afraid that it would not be "right." She could not answer in class. She could not hand in written work.
—Teacher of gifted students

Alicia was under the care of a clinical psychologist. Her psychologist, parents, teachers, and counselor knew that she was capable of functioning at an extremely high intellectual level. They persuaded her to enroll in a seminar designed for gifted students, hoping that she would eventually respond to the special teaching strategies and peer support. Everyone encouraged Alicia, despite occasional feelings of doubt. One day in class, Alicia tentatively raised her hand. By the end of the semester, Alicia was responding to the intellectual stimulation provided by her teacher and classmates. She was able to turn in assignments and participate in class discussions. When Alicia applied to college 3 years later, her application was accepted.

> In seventh grade, Jason scored 1500 out of 1600 on the SAT. His grades, however, were mediocre. The only thing he seemed to care about was computers and computer games. It was obvious that he didn't have to put forth any effort to earn high grades; however, he didn't seem to care and frequently didn't hand in assignments. He seemed to need a sense of purpose.
>
> —Parent of a gifted student

When Jason applied to college, his transcript reflected a series of ups and downs—grades that ranged from A to F. His grade point average was less than remarkable, reflecting his tendency either to turn in work that teachers considered brilliant, or not turn in his assignments at all. His standardized test scores reflected high ability and high aptitude in all areas. His test scores included grades of 4 and 5 on AP Examinations, and he had entered a national mathematics competition, where he excelled.

Jason's parents and teachers thought of him as brilliant, but unmotivated. His guidance counselor described him as "an unharnessed dynamo." When he applied to college, his application was rejected everywhere. His guidance counselor called several colleges and discovered that Jason was identified as a risky applicant, in part because he had high scores on standardized tests and a low grade point average (GPA). The counselor, having spent several years persuading Jason to remain in high school, decided to argue on his behalf. The counselor was successful, and Jason was admitted to a highly selective college. Although Jason's college grades were less than admirable and he continued to feel frustrated with educational structure, he earned a college degree. The guidance counselor's support provided Jason with an opportunity to take one step toward fulfilling his potential.

> It was difficult to convince Anna, age 15, to take AP courses. She felt she could not succeed academically and continue to help support her family.
> —Guidance Counselor

Anna's parents, who were culturally diverse, struggled to earn a living. When Anna was recommended for AP courses, her family objected. The expectations of high academic achievement and postsecondary education on the part of both the teachers and students were different from those of her family and neighbors. Her father expected that Anna would complete high school and work in the family grocery store. Her mother worried that Anna would lose her cultural identity if she enrolled in highly rigorous courses. Despite family protests, Anna took advantage of every academic opportunity. When she applied to college, her family argued that she should enroll in the local community college, in part because they knew they could not afford tuition, room, and board anywhere else. Her counselor argued that Anna could attend any college she wanted. Several highly selective colleges accepted Anna. Her counselor watched for possible scholarships and, whenever possible, argued the merits of Anna's case.

The above vignettes are examples of students who were labeled *underachieving* during high school. These gifted students are quite different from one another. They do, however, share two attributes: their potential and a counselor, teacher, or parent who recognized that potential and decided to encourage the student.

If your child exhibits many of these characteristics consistently and for more than 1 year, he or she may be underachieving in school:

- inattentiveness;
- disorganization;
- does homework carelessly or incompletely;

- "forgets" to turn in assignments even they are when completed;
- procrastinates until the night before;
- disruptive in some classes;
- argumentative;
- asks for more help than necessary;
- blames others;
- makes excuses;
- avoids competition;
- considers school boring; or
- interest in learning has declined in school, as well as at home.

The idea of an underachieving gifted student is seen by many to be an oxymoron. How can a student be gifted and not succeed in school? Research studies often raise more questions than they answer. These students do not live up to expectations, causing their parents and teachers frustration. But, whose expectations are they not living up to? Is potential measurable or, in the words of Charlie Brown, is potential the "world's heaviest burden?" Are we describing gifted students who are experiencing academic difficulty and feel uncomfortable, or are we describing parents, teachers, or counselors who expect more than a student is willing and able to produce?

Underachieving gifted students are often described in terms of significant inconsistencies in measured ability and grades earned in school. For example, Jason was identified as gifted at an early age through the use of the Wechsler Intelligence Scale for Children (WISC-IV). His standardized test scores reflected high ability and aptitude in all areas; however, he earned mediocre grades in many high school subjects.

Some students are silent underachievers—no one knows how capable they are because they haven't had opportunities to demonstrate their advanced reasoning. Students whose capabilities are a total mismatch with the curriculum may not be recognized as gifted (Baum, 1990; Delisle & Berger, 1990). We may not know the ability level of a particular student who camouflages giftedness under satisfactory

39

performance, especially if the student's teachers, counselor, and parents have no evidence to indicate that the student is gifted. Many gifted students with disabilities fit into this group of underachievers—giftedness and the learning disability mask one another. Some of these students may have been recognized as having a disability, but no one recognized their potential. Or, they may have been recognized as gifted, but could not negotiate an expanded curriculum.

Specific personality traits and behaviors such as impulsiveness, lack of motivation, inability to concentrate for long periods of time, deficiencies in specific skills, inconsistent work habits, perfectionism, fear of failure, and social isolation have also been identified and viewed as both an influence on and an effect of long-term underachievement (Janos & Robinson, 1985; Rimm, 1986; Whitmore, 1980, 1986). Some of these characteristics and behaviors, however, have been observed in eminent adults. An analysis of autobiographies such as *Surely You're Joking, Mr. Feynman!* (Feynman, 1985) and *The Autobiography of Eleanor Roosevelt* (Roosevelt, 1958) indicates that eminent adults who have made significant contributions to society share some of these characteristics. Underachievement cannot be understood when approached solely from the perspective of student characteristics; rather, the problem is multidimensional.

Most experts believe that underachievement is related to a number of factors, some within the child, some within the environment, and some due to a mismatch of the two (Reis & McCoach, 2002). Most interventions have been met with limited success, and were designed for immediate results with a population of severely underachieving children (Supplee, 1990; Whitmore, 1980). These interventions consist of carefully crafted environments with a smaller teacher-student ratio and highly trained teachers.

Felice Kaufmann, a researcher and educator with extensive experience working with gifted students, believes that underachievement is a defensive behavior that protects against feelings of profound discouragement. Kaufmann has described underachieving gifted students as discouraged individuals who need encouragement, but tend to reject praise as artificial or inauthentic. Excessive praise may strengthen the underachiever's belief that she is acceptable only when she is doing something that is valued by others. In other words, "cheerleading" is unlikely to provide these students with the necessary ammunition to cope with their problems (F. Kaufmann, personal communication, August 1989). She found that underachieving gifted students have difficulty committing work to paper, tend to lack confidence, avoid responsibility, avoid competition, may be highly resistant to adult and peer influence, and may be highly perfectionistic, sensitive, and vulnerable. These students may respond to counseling, although counseling too has been met with limited success. Often, the counselor's goal is to help the student decide whether academic achievement is a desired aspiration (Reis & McCoach, 2002).

College planning for an underachieving gifted student is a bit of a conundrum, because it involves a match between student needs and school offerings. An underachiever is going to have a difficult time making that match. On the one hand, gifted students are motivated by and need topics that interest them. They respond positively to appropriate instructional strategies. Selective schools are unlikely to view an underachieving student as a match for their offerings. Often, that leaves the student with four options: (1) a small private college with counseling available as part of the curriculum; (2) a 2-year community college where a student can learn to work at a more challenging level for a couple of years and then transfer to a 4-year school; (3) an additional year of secondary school at a private school before moving into a collegiate environment; or (4) an internship or volunteer position where the student can spend time providing a needed service. Many students choose to do a postgraduate year at a private school to improve their chances for admission to a selective or highly selective college. A postgraduate year is beneficial for strengthening academic skills and may give students a chance to mature. Some students enroll in community colleges to raise their GPA. Community colleges do not usually provide an appropriate peer group for gifted students or an appropriate level of instruction. Without coun-

41

seling, the student may repeat the same patterns as in high school. Private high schools are expensive, with very little financial aid available. Lists of private schools that offer a postgraduate year can often be found online using a search engine.

What Parents Can Do

As your gifted student approaches adolescence and high school, you may become increasingly concerned about achievement. Simultaneously, your child may experience internal and external conflicts while attempting to establish a separate identity. You can help by creating and maintaining a mutually respectful atmosphere, helping your child establish effective priorities, defining sensible guidelines, and acting as a guide on the side, rather than a sage on the stage. There are many instances where we know a great deal more than our students and tell them so—like a sage on the stage. But, it may be much better to have a respectful conversation, gently guiding students, even when we think we know best. With that in mind, the following suggestions may be useful:

- A student who experiences a sudden academic decline in one or two subjects during the junior or senior year is probably not an underachiever. This student, however, will need to explain the drop in grades on a college application. When it is handled properly, such an event may be turned into an asset. This idea will be discussed in more detail in Chapter 5.
- Talk about the future on a regular basis. Instead of talking about the need to be admitted to a good college, talk to your child about life beyond the undergraduate years. Discuss the joys and downsides of your own career. Encourage your child to form some ideas about her own future. She should be discouraged from saying "I have no idea," when someone asks her what she wants to do in her future. She can change her mind 200 times, but having only a cloudy view of the future is not a positive sign.
- Some students are more interested in learning than in working for grades. Such a student might spend hours

on a project that is unrelated to academic classes and fail to turn in required work. This inner-directed student should be strongly encouraged to pursue his or her interests, particularly because those interests often lead to lifelong career satisfaction. Simultaneously, the student should be reminded that teachers might be unsympathetic when required work is incomplete. Comprehensive career planning emphasizing short- and long-term goals often helps such a student to complete required assignments, pass high school courses, and plan for college.

• Help kids develop coping strategies. They should know how to deal with setbacks, stresses, and feelings of inadequacy. They should also learn how to solve problems and resolve conflicts, and learn ways to brainstorm and think critically.

• Provide an accepting environment, positive feedback, reasonable rules and guidelines, strong support, and encouragement by recognizing effort, progress, and improvement. Avoid overemphasizing achievement.

• Maintain your objectivity and sense of humor. Parental caring, understanding, and objectivity are critical resources for gifted students to be used as armor when faced with insensitive people, embarrassment, or humiliation.

• Listen to your gifted student. Show genuine interest in his or her observations, interests, activities, and goals. Be sensitive to problems, but avoid transmitting unrealistic or conflicting expectations and solving problems the student is capable of managing.

• Guide your adolescent toward activities and goals that reflect his or her values, interests, and needs, not yours.

• Encourage your student to acquire a wide variety of experiences, particularly those that will assist him in college and career planning. For example, if your son is interested in politics, suggest that he volunteer to work in a campaign office. Your child may benefit from such an experience in two ways: (1) by feeling useful for providing a service to the community without thought of

43

compensation; and (2) by knowing and understanding a realistic view of the work world.

- Share your perspective on how you successfully handle stressful situations, disappointment, and discouragement. Underachieving gifted students are frequently idealistic and believe that no one else shares their problems.
- Get involved in your child's school. Volunteer your time. Although your student may be less than appreciative, counselors and teachers need and value your assistance and support. You may also acquire useful information that will help you assist your adolescent.
- Search for a group of parents who can provide a support system. Parent advocacy groups for gifted students exist in many communities and offer a network for communication, information, and assistance. In lieu of a local group, contact the National Association for Gifted Children (http://www.nagc.org).
- Avoid overinvesting in your child's achievement level.
- Avoid discouraging comments, such as "If you're so gifted, why did you get a D in _____?" or "I've given you everything; why are you so _____?"
- Keep in mind that some students are extremely unhappy in secondary school and do not do well academically (in part because of the organization and structure). These students, however, may handle independence quite well; they may be extremely happy and successful in the right college when learning in an environment with a different structural organization.
- Some students are underachievers because they do not have the opportunity to use what they know. This is frequently true of musicians and students with technical abilities. If this describes your teen, find an environment where he or she will feel successful.
- Search for appropriate summer activities that the student will enjoy, particularly those that deal with the student's interests. Some underachieving gifted students develop a love of learning through summer courses and activities, and the love of learning, unlike grades, lasts a lifetime.

- Provide appropriate college and career guidance by exposing your teen to work environments. Internships usually work well if the student has control over the place and time he works. Some students benefit from a residential college planning seminar offered by many colleges.
- Avoid praise and artificial compliments. These comments may not resonate with the way the student feels internally. Recognize effort and improvement rather than the final product.

The College Search:
A Matter of Matching

3

C ollege planning for gifted students is about making a match between the gifted student's goals, interests, and needs and a college's offerings. Knowing oneself is a critical part of that matching process. When your adolescent begins to compile a list of colleges for consideration, usually sometime during 11th grade, his self-knowledge and experiences should govern his choices. Although that sounds like conventional wisdom, most students make arbitrary decisions about college, in part because they don't know what they want and don't know how to find out. They don't realize that colleges vary by size, location, student diversity, extracurricular activities, and programs of study. Many teens have not reflected on their strengths, interests, and needs. Before making that all-important list of colleges, chosen because they are a match for interests and preferences, your adolescent should begin to answer these questions.

- Who am I—what are my values, attitudes, beliefs, interests?
- What's important to me—family, career, religion, power, money, social life, music, arts, sports?
- Where do I want to live for 4 years—large city, suburbs, rural area?
- Which academic subjects do I like best and least?

- How do I learn best—reading, talking, independently, self-paced, seminar, lecture, hands-on?
- Why do I want to go to college?

The last question may be the most important. A student who wants to party should probably apply to a school that is very different from the student who wants to study with a well-known professor. A student who has a passion for English literature may choose a school that is very different from the one chosen by a computer wizard who wants to specialize in microbiology. The student questionnaire, "Why Are You Going to College?" on page 49 gives students an idea of the type of college they should look for.

Knowing Oneself

The years from the beginning of 7th grade to the end of 12th grade are turbulent times for all adolescents, particularly gifted adolescents. During this critical period, your child will try on many personalities that will blend into his self-awareness. Hopefully, your teen will learn to use his or her talents in constructive, satisfying ways, and develop an appreciation for his or her community. Your child needs to discover, explore, investigate, and participate in different types of activities, intellectual ideas, academic disciplines, extracurricular activities, and social relationships. To accomplish this, he should be exposed to and participate in many different types of activities. Middle school and high school are meant for exploration, growing intellectually, finding interests and passions, and learning to accept challenges. It is also important for your child to begin to develop effective writing skills, an essential skill in high school and college. Students learn a great deal about themselves each time they participate in anything new and develop new skills.

Understanding oneself depends, in part, on one's breadth and depth of experience, because it is through experience that we know what we like and what we dislike. This section of the book includes many different types of academic

Student Questionnaire: Why Are You Going to College?

Many colleges and universities offer a well-rounded education, an escape from home, and the time and opportunity to pursue abilities and interests. But, if you take a closer look at why you are going to college, you will get a better idea of how selective you should be in your search. There are 25 statements listed below. Check off the 5 statements that most accurately describe your reasons for going to college. They are not listed in any particular order.

My reasons for going to college include:

_____ 1. To live in a different part of the country.

_____ 2. To be exposed to new ideas.

_____ 3. To have a more interesting social life.

_____ 4. To be near cultural activities.

_____ 5. To get practical experience in my chosen field.

_____ 6. To prepare for a specific professional school (e.g., law, architecture, dentistry, or medicine).

_____ 7. To get a solid liberal arts background.

_____ 8. To participate in athletic activities.

_____ 9. To be challenged academically.

_____10. To compete with others on my level.

_____11. To go to a high-status school.

_____12. To get specific vocational or career training.

_____13. To help me get a good job or career.

Student Questionnaire: Why Are You Going to College?, continued

_____14. To meet people different from myself.

_____15. To study and live abroad.

_____16. To take classes from renowned professors.

_____17. To develop my abilities, potential, talents, and interests.

_____18. To participate in a special educational program.

_____19. To be out on my own.

_____20. To join in extracurricular activities.

_____21. To earn a better living and have a better lifestyle.

_____22. To satisfy my parents.

_____23. To go where my friends are going.

_____24. Because I have nothing better to do.

_____25. To have fun and not work too hard for the next 2 to 4 years.

If you checked off numbers 2, 3, 8, 17, 19, 22, 24, or 25, almost any college can offer you the right opportunities. If you chose numbers 1, 4, 5, 7, 9, 10, 12, 13, 14, 15, 18, 20, 21, or 23, you will have to be more selective. If numbers 6, 11, or 16 were among your choices, you will have to look for a highly competitive and academically prestigious school.

and nonacademic opportunities that will send your child on an exploratory journey toward an expanding self-awareness. Almost any activity can be a source of enrichment for your son or daughter. However, a highly enriching activity will bring some intrinsic, as well as extrinsic rewards in the form of self-confidence and a growing sense of self. Summer is usually the most convenient time your teen can take a course and investigate new topics. Colleges are very interested as to how adolescents spend their free time, because it's a way to tell the difference between two equally deserving candidates. If a college admissions reader sees that your child spent her free time wisely—learning, sharing talents, and exhibiting leadership—the reader is likely to award her extra points. However, if the reader sees that a child spent the summer acquiring a suntan, the candidate becomes less appealing. If a student has to work during the summer in order to save up for college expenses, it should be stated on the application, so as not to be misleading.

Self-Knowledge Goals

The ingredients of self-knowledge for adolescents are self-exploration, academic planning, intellectual and social/emotional enrichment, decision-making skills (how to analyze and evaluate alternatives), and effective work and study skills, including time management. Before students reach the active portion of college planning, the part that involves looking at colleges, they should know something about their interests and, in particular, what they want from a college. The questionnaire on page 49 will help determine that. The answers may change as students get older, and that's OK.

Many students have not thought about what truly interests them. Of course, interests change as we age, but knowing and pursuing the topics and activities that interest you can help you shape your future. Having your child complete an interest inventory is a way for him to start thinking about how his interests relate to his future. Middle school students can complete the middle school interest inventory on page 52–53, while high school students should complete the one presented on pages 54–55.

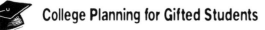
Personal Interest Inventory for Middle School Students

The following questions will help you begin to know yourself better. (It works better if you write down the answers so you can reflect on them.) There are no right or wrong answers, and the answers may change over time. Add your own questions to this list.

1. What kinds of books do you like to read? _____

   _____

2. What parts of the newspaper do you read? _____

   _____

3. How do you know what is happening in the world around you? _

   _____

4. What TV programs do you enjoy? _____

   _____

5. What do you like to do when you have free time? _____

   _____

6. What is your favorite subject in school? Why? _____

   _____

7. What don't you like to do in school? Why? _____

   _____

8. What kinds of things do you like to collect? _____

   _____

9. What do you see yourself doing in 5 years? 10 years? _____

   _____

10. If you could talk to any historical figure, who would you choose? What three questions would you ask? _____

    _____

    _____

Personal Interest Inventory for Middle School Students, continued

11. If you could learn about anything in school this year, what would you choose? _____

_____

12. Think about the skills you are most proud of. Which of those skills would you like to improve this year? _____

_____

13. Think about your interests: What do you like to do? Think about experiences you have enjoyed. _____

_____

14. What kind of school, religious, social, or sports activities do you like?

_____

_____

_____

15. Make a list of 10 specific activities you have enjoyed doing in the past 4 years. _____

_____

_____

_____

_____

16. Think about what you liked about the activities. What challenges did the activities offer? What skills do you need to develop further to continue in those activities? _____

_____

_____

_____

_____

Eventually you will understand how interests and skills connect for you. Everyone is different. You need to find your own path.

53

Interest Inventory for High School Students

This activity is designed to show you how to define or create jobs that incorporate your interests. Place a checkmark next to every item that you really like to do or want to learn to do in the next few months.

- ___ study nature
- ___ be outdoors
- ___ rearrange furniture
- ___ decorate things
- ___ collect things
- ___ listen to music
- ___ travel to new places
- ___ take care of young children
- ___ solve problems
- ___ work with numbers
- ___ raise funds for causes
- ___ work on machines/cars
- ___ grow plants and flowers
- ___ meet people
- ___ read the Bible
- ___ build things
- ___ analyze systems
- ___ study languages and words
- ___ engage in business activities
- ___ teach others
- ___ keep records/bookkeeping
- ___ explore new places
- ___ sing
- ___ speak in public
- ___ exchange ideas
- ___ conserve natural resources
- ___ draw, paint, or sketch
- ___ study art
- ___ work with details
- ___ be around animals
- ___ do scientific research
- ___ be around the media
- ___ read for pleasure
- ___ analyze movies
- ___ design things
- ___ plan budgets

- ___ join public causes
- ___ talk about politics
- ___ do electrical work
- ___ study stocks and investments
- ___ data processing
- ___ read novels
- ___ science fiction
- ___ visit forests and streams
- ___ write poetry and stories
- ___ sell things
- ___ supervise people
- ___ operate a computer
- ___ observe human behavior
- ___ church activities
- ___ work with my hands
- ___ understand how things work
- ___ create new things
- ___ read philosophy
- ___ dissect an organism
- ___ dance
- ___ ballet
- ___ bird watch
- ___ anticipate needs of others
- ___ visit older people
- ___ socialize at parties
- ___ care for sick people
- ___ give advice
- ___ plan events
- ___ study artifacts
- ___ use a microscope
- ___ act in a play
- ___ play individual sports
- ___ play team sports
- ___ other _____

Interest Inventory for High School Students, continued

Review those interests you have just checked and select four you would like to have in your future paid employment. (Some interests develop into careers and some interests develop into leisure activities or hobbies.) Taking these interests one at a time, visualize the activities and settings that you associate with each. After seeing these pictures in your mind, imagine ways in which you could combine all four into a job. Don't concern yourself with job titles at this point. Focus on describing tasks that combine all four interests. There are no right or wrong answers. This is just for you.

The four interests I might want in my work are

_____, _____,

_____, _____.

Example 1: Suppose your interests include: designing things, anticipating the needs of others, writing prose, and planning events. What future work settings might you imagine?

_____

_____

_____

_____

Example 2: Suppose your interests include listening to music, analyzing movies, playing tennis, and socializing at parties. What future work settings might you imagine?

_____

_____

_____

_____

55

Sources of Enrichment and Summer Opportunities

Does your son or daughter have a passion to work side by side with a microbiologist 8 hours a day, or collaborate with playwrights and directors to produce a new play? Be immersed in the world of music? Write for 12 hours a day, creating short stories, poems, essays, or a weekly newspaper? Study the ecosystems of coral reefs on daily dives in the Caribbean? Build a wooden sea kayak and paddle it along the Maine coast for 3 weeks? Learn to speak Arabic, Chinese, or Portuguese? These are all possible pursuits during the summer months.

During the next few years, there is likely to be a time when your gifted child wants to learn something entirely new, like psychology, creative writing, archaeology, or genealogy. A typical school day does not leave time for exploring a topic in depth, or playing with ideas. Teachers must follow a state-approved syllabus, which can be very confining. If your child is gifted but does not participate in a gifted program, he or she may have few true peers. Finding an appropriate summer enrichment opportunity might provide a good solution. There are literally hundreds of places to look for enrichment. Every state has a university that offers enrichment to high school students during the summer. The regional talent search programs are a good source, as is your own school district. Lots of school districts offer fee-based summer enrichment classes. Some school districts sponsor overseas travel.

We live in a world where there is so much to do that it's sometimes hard to decide what we want. We have a lot of choices, as do our children. Do we want to improve skills? Develop new skills? Help someone less fortunate? To find summer programs other than those offered by talent search organizations, check out the directory listings on the Center for Talented Youth at Johns Hopkins University Web site (http://www.jhu.edu/gifted).

Some gifted students tend to take on too many activities and commitments. As a parent, you can tell when your child is overextended and stressed, and if you see that happening during the summer, eliminate some activities so that your child has less to cope with. This does not mean that students should be encouraged to devote their summer months solely to catching up on soap operas or mastering the newest video game—just that they should do something stimulating and interesting *and* take time to relax.

Parents and students should consider the following questions when discussing enrichment opportunities:

- What are the adolescent's intellectual, social, and emotional needs?
- How does a particular enrichment opportunity match those needs?
- What new opportunities will benefit your teen and what does he or she want to do?
- How does the cost of a program compare to the services and resources provided, and is scholarship money available from the program or outside organizations?

The following publications and organizations provide lists and descriptions of enrichment programs for gifted and talented students:

- *Educational Opportunity Guide: A Directory of Programs for the Gifted* (available at http://www.tip.duke.edu)
  Programs are categorized by state and cross-referenced by categories such as programs for minority students only and free, non-state-supported programs. Included are programs administered by Duke University's Talent Identification Program (TIP) and other regional talent searches and programs administered by other universities in cooperation with regional talent searches.
- *Summer Opportunities for Kids & Teenagers 2006* (available at http://www.petersons.com)
  Lists almost 3,000 national and international summer programs, tours, and service projects.
- National Association for Gifted Children (NAGC) searchable database of summer programs (available at

57

http://www.nagc.org; be sure to click on the Resource Directory tab)

When perusing this list, keep in mind that to be included, programs must pay a fee, which may limit some programs from participating.

Above-Grade-Level Testing

Above-grade-level testing means taking a standardized test that is meant for considerably older students. Young students may find it valuable to assess their abilities compared with much older students. The major college entrance tests are the SAT and ACT, which are both frequently taken by seventh- and eighth-grade students. Some talent search programs offer standardized tests geared to students who are younger than seventh grade, such as the EXPLORE test of the American College Testing (ACT) program and the PLUS test of the Educational Testing Service (ETS). Both tests may offer students a way of understanding their intellectual and academic strengths and weaknesses and give them time to improve their weaker areas before reaching high school. Information about either of these tests is available from your closest regional talent search program or ACT and ETS.

Regional Talent Searches and Cooperative Programs

The term *talent search* refers to a specific type of educational program for gifted and advanced learners held within the United States. All of the talent searches are located regionally; their service areas range from single-state searches to quite large ones. The largest regional talent search programs are the Center for Talented Youth at Johns Hopkins University (CTY), the Talent Identification Program at Duke University (TIP), the Northwestern University Center for Talent Development (CTD), and the Rocky Mountain Talent Search at the University of Denver (RMTS). Although the four programs have unique features, each conducts its talent search in basically the same way. Seventh- and eighth-grade students who score at the 95th percentile or above on a standardized achievement test register to take the SAT or the ACT in the fall. These tests are typically taken by high school students preparing to attend college, which is why they are called *out-of-level* or *above-grade-level* tests. The talent search programs use the SAT and ACT, because they provide a better measure of intellectual abilities than standardized achievement tests designed for the middle school level. Participating in the testing can provide the young teen with an assessment of his or her abilities, compared with those of students who are high school juniors or seniors. (The scores of students who are below ninth grade are not reported to colleges when you take the tests later, unless you choose to do so.) Based on students' scores on the SAT or ACT, various kinds of educational options and experiences, ranging from high-level enrichment courses, to subject and grade acceleration, are recommended.

The talent search includes three important components: (1) diagnosis and evaluation of levels of talent; (2) educational placement and guidance; and (3) talent development opportunities including summer programs, distance learning programs, contests, and competitions.

All of this occurs for more than 150,000 students from the ages of 13–14 each year (Olszewski-Kubilius, 1995). Qualified students may be invited to participate in summer residential programs or commuter programs or take advantage of other academic opportunities. The programs also offer college and career planning assistance. Talent search opportunities have taken many different forms: fast-paced summer classes and Saturday programs, early access to AP courses, enrollment of junior high students in high school courses, dual enrollment of high school students in college classes, correspondence courses for high school and college-level courses, and early entrance programs for college. Each of the four universities that conduct a regional talent search produces a compendium of educational programs within its region, and the number of programs grows annually.

59

An outgrowth of the regional talent search is the Elementary Student Talent Search (for grades 3–6), offered by Carnegie Mellon University, Northwestern University, the University of Iowa, and Duke University, as well as the Young Students Talent Search (grades 5 and 6) offered by Johns Hopkins University. The requirements for participation include scoring at the 95th percentile on grade-level standardized tests.

The goals of all of the programs include the following:

- to identify academically talented young people,
- to inform them of their abilities and academic options,
- to sponsor challenging educational programs, and
- to develop an effective research effort to help understand the nature of academically talented adolescents (Johns Hopkins University Center for Talented Youth, n.d.a).

Additional goals and specific provisions depend on the individual program.

Courses offered by talent search programs are specifically designed to challenge students with high ability. Directors of national talent searches point out the following intellectual and social/emotional advantages of these programs:

- Students who tend to concentrate on specific academic disciplines (e.g., mathematics and science) are encouraged to explore previously undiscovered disciplines such as philosophy, anthropology, or psychology.
- Students who require academic acceleration can choose from a wide variety of courses that might not be available in their local high schools.
- Students establish and maintain relationships with other adolescents who share their abilities, views, and interests. This is particularly important for gifted students, because they frequently feel isolated.
- Students receive information on college and career planning.
- Students who have participated in regional talent search programs and other university-based institutes say that friendships established during the summer continue years later.

Why should students participate in talent searches? Talent searches provide students with a better measure of their abilities, allow them to become eligible for educational opportunities (such as summer classes, informational mailings, and career symposia), and provide them with information that is useful in educational placement and guidance.

If your student is eligible for educational opportunities and summer enrichment through a regional talent search, keep in mind that participation in the program is not required. You can simply say to yourself, "Now I know that he or she is eligible" and drop the idea. However, if your teen participates and takes a course that might require a high school schedule change, you should tell the high school before they make up student schedules. For example, if your student takes algebra during the summer and will require geometry in the fall, don't wait until the last minute to tell your child's guidance counselor.

Governor's School Programs

Governor's School residential programs provide intensive high-quality programs that focus on diverse areas (e.g., arts or academic disciplines such as science). Many states offer a residential Governor's School program only to students who are between their junior and senior year. Specific criteria for selection of students differ, depending on the state. In some states, local educators nominate students, but in many states, a student may inform a teacher or guidance counselor that he or she wants to be considered for nomination. In other states, students may contact the program directly and request nomination. Specific program goals also vary by state, but all programs recognize academic excellence and artistic or leadership ability. For general information about Governor's Schools, visit the National Conference of Governor's Schools Web site at http://ncogs.org.

Mentor Relationships

One of the most valuable experiences a high school student can have is exposure to a mentor who is willing to share his or her personal values, particular interests, time, talents, and skills. When the mentor is a good match for your child, the relationship can provide both your daughter and her mentor with encouragement, inspiration, new insights, and other personal rewards. Many students find mentors while participating in talent search programs or high school internships. Internships are valuable because they allow a student to investigate a potential career interest. A mentorship, on the other hand, is a relationship in which values, attitudes, passions, and traditions are passed from one person to another and internalized.

The benefits of having a mentor ultimately affect a student's choice of career and salary. In terms of career advancement, particularly for women, mentors make a huge difference. Presidential Scholars are selected from the brightest 12th-grade students in the nation. In a study of Presidential Scholars 15 years after these students graduated from high school, they were asked questions that pertained to the nature, role, and influence of their most significant mentors. Although not everyone had a mentor, those who did said that having a role model, and the support and encouragement of a mentor were the biggest benefits (Kaufmann, 1981; Kaufmann, Harrel, Milam, Woolverton, & Miller, 1986). Mentors set an example, offered intellectual stimulation, communicated excitement and joy in the learning process, and understood these students and their needs.

The research also revealed the critical importance of mentors for gifted girls (Kaufmann et al., 1986). In this study, the earning power of the women and men was compared, and it was discovered that there was a salary gap between men and women in the same profession who shared the same credentials. The men were paid more for the same work. However, when the earning powers of the women were equal to those of the men, it was discovered that those women had had one or more mentors. In other words, the presence of a mentor may equalize earning power (Kaufmann, 1981; Kaufmann et al.).

Educators, counselors, and parents can all help gifted students find mentors. The following questions may help you decide whether to pursue this approach:

- Does the student want a mentor? Or, does the student simply want exposure to a particular subject or career field?
- Is the student prepared to spend a significant amount of time working with the mentor?
- Does the student understand the purpose, benefits, and limitations of the mentor relationship?

To identify mentor candidates, contact local businesses, universities, professional associations, and organizations such as the American Association of Retired Persons. Your child may want to focus on working on a significant and specific project with his or her mentor. Such projects can later be submitted for recognition by competitions and contests, and the experience of working on the project can also provide a valuable asset in college applications, essays, and interviews.

You also can look for mentors on the Internet, as long as you look for mentors from legitimate organizations. If you can identify some candidates, you may want to ask the following questions:

- Does the mentor understand and like working with gifted adolescents?
- Is the mentor willing to be a real role model, sharing the excitement and joy of learning?
- Is the mentor's teaching style compatible with the student's learning style?

Community Service and Volunteer Activities

Students need to learn how to share their talents freely with others. When we help others, we learn much about ourselves and make our own lives more meaningful. This can be accomplished in many ways. You might suggest that your student volunteer at a local nursing home or a hospital, or share a specific talent with young children. For example, teens can coach a local children's athletic team or teach computer programming to low-income students. The focus of the volunteer work will depend on your child's talent and available resources. Your teen's school might institute a volunteer program, such as the one held annually at a Virginia magnet school, which helps its students find opportunities to share their talents. At the Virginia school, community service is a graduation requirement. A wide variety of activities are offered, and the students are highly enthusiastic about their service opportunities. They volunteer for activities such as tutoring younger children, reading to older persons, and participating in political campaigns. Students can also learn about many careers by volunteering their time to businesses and nonprofit organizations.

Travel

There are many significant benefits to exposing your child to other environments and cultures, in the U.S. or in other countries. You can introduce your child to a dynamic learning environment in which knowledge is accumulated through direct contact with other cultures. School systems throughout the nation sponsor overseas travel during the summer, preceded by several weeks of classes where students absorb some of the history and culture of the country where they plan to travel. Selected teachers and parents often serve as chaperones. If classes are offered prior to and following summer travel, students are introduced to the country to be visited and encouraged to discuss their experiences when they return. Some school systems award credit for participation in these institutes. For a database of study abroad programs, check out http//www.studyabroad.com.

Advanced Academics

While colleges are concerned with the outside enrichment opportunities a student undertakes to explore her interests, their primary concern remains her ability to be successful under stressful, challenging academic conditions. Taking advanced-level classes and challenging oneself academically is a good way to show colleges that a student is ready for college-level work.

Some gifted students will be attracted to highly selective colleges, schools that reject more applications than they accept. The most selective colleges look for evidence of high student motivation and achievement—good grades in very demanding courses. They expect to see AP courses on the student's transcript, if these courses are provided by the student's high school. Planning for advanced courses must begin as early as the eighth or ninth grade, especially in the case of sequential courses such as mathematics. For instance, the progression to AP calculus requires several years of prerequisite courses beginning with algebra. The same kind of planning is necessary for languages and sciences. Some students will not be ready or able to begin an advanced mathematics, foreign language, or science sequence by eighth grade. In such cases, courses offered during the summer or correspondence courses sponsored by regional talent search programs may be a viable option.

Advanced Placement Courses

AP courses offer gifted high school students the opportunity to broaden their depth and scope of learning in one or more subjects of interest, pursue college-level studies while still enrolled in secondary school, and demonstrate their capacity to handle college-level work. Students enrolled in AP courses may develop study skills that match or exceed those of college freshmen. To earn college credit, students take the AP Examination, a 3-hour comprehensive test in an individual subject area. Good exam results can be parlayed into college credits and permissions to advance directly to higher level courses. Students must choose carefully when taking the exams. A fee is charged for each test, and studying for AP tests takes a lot of time. They should know what they would gain from taking each test (College Board AP Central,

65

n.d.). If they are already taking three or four exams, perhaps taking that fifth exam may not make sense.

When looking at colleges, students should keep in mind that some colleges offer exemption, credit, or both for AP Exam grades of 3, 4, or 5. Because most high schools calculate a student's overall GPA differently from others, many colleges recalculate the GPA, often taking into account the academic rigor of the courses on a transcript. If a student is seriously interested in a college, she should be sure to ask about course credit and ask how the college's admissions staff weighs AP tests.

AP Exams are offered each May at participating schools to students who want to be tested at the college level in areas such as English, calculus, science, computer science, history, foreign languages, art, and music. AP courses and examinations now cover 35 subjects, including art history, economics (micro and macro), and studio art (2-D and 3-D design), and they are taken by more than a million students from 11,000 public and 4,000 other schools, including those in other countries (Mollison, 2006). A student need not be enrolled in an AP course in order to take the exam. AP tests are graded on a scale from 1 to 5 (5 is the highest score). Grades of 3, 4, or 5 on AP Exams may be considered acceptable for college credit or exemption from required courses. Exemption or AP credit varies among colleges and is offered at the discretion of each college (College Board AP Central, n.d.).

Many states receive a grant to enable them to reimburse low-income individuals for part or all of the cost of AP test fees if those low-income individuals (a) are enrolled in an AP class, and (b) plan to take an AP test. Contact your state education agency or board of education for more information.

Each college or university decides how much credit, if any, will be awarded to the student depending on the test score. Many highly selective colleges will accept only a score of 5 for credit. To find colleges that offer AP credit or placement, visit the College Board's Web site (http://www.collegeboard.com). If a student takes an AP test, the student is responsible for ensuring that the scores reach the college. For additional information about AP Programs, visit the College Board's AP Central at http://ap central.collegeboard.com.

The College Board provides broad outlines of course content and examination methods. However, the specific curriculum content of AP courses is determined by each school or school district and taught by high school teachers. This means that there will be some inconsistencies in the quality of courses and the preparedness of teachers, although everyone takes the same AP Examination in a specific topic. However, the Duke University Talent Identification Program (TIP) has developed and published a series of AP teacher's manuals designed to assist local educators to develop and organize a new AP course, enhance an already existing AP course, introduce fresh ideas to honors-level courses, and produce educationally rich units for regular classroom instruction (Duke University TIP, 2005).

Honors Versus Advanced Placement Courses

Many secondary schools throughout the country offer both an AP program and an Honors program. Because students often have to choose between the programs, it's important for parents, as well as students, to understand the difference.

The AP Program consists of courses in a wide variety of subject areas developed by both high school and college faculty under the auspices of the College Board. The courses cover the breadth of information, skills, and assignments found in corresponding college courses. Most U.S. colleges and universities, as well as colleges and universities in 28 other countries, have an AP policy granting incoming students credit, placement, or both on the basis of their grades on AP Exams. Many of these institutions grant up to a full year of college credit (sophomore standing) to students who earn a sufficient number of qualifying AP grades. There have been several research studies that looked at what students gain by taking an AP course and taking an AP Examination. It makes sense that students who take the course and score well on the exam have a better chance at succeeding in college and

67

graduating on time (in 4 years; Mollison, 2006). But, what about the students who take the course, take the exam, and do not score well? Surprisingly, researchers have discovered that even these students benefit from the rigor in studying for the exam. It's possible that the effort prepares them for college examinations, even though they did not score well (Mathews, 2005).

Honors classes differ from AP courses in several ways. First, they are developed locally by district teachers to meet the needs of high-achieving students. Second, most honors classes offer the same curriculum offered in the corresponding regular, nonhonors classes at the school, but the honors classes are designed to be more challenging by covering additional topics or some topics in greater depth. Most students and parents want to know whether AP courses are more difficult than honors classes. The answer is usually yes; however, difficult is a relative concept, so the answer really depends on the nature of the honors courses and the standards upheld in those courses.

Students should understand that unlike AP courses, honors courses won't earn them college credit, but there are still important benefits. For example, colleges will recognize a student's willingness to challenge himself academically. Honors courses also prepare students for college-level work, and the more prepared students are, the greater their chances for success. Be sure that your child's high school transcripts indicate a course as honors—particularly if it's not part of the transcript course description—so colleges easily recognize honors courses students have taken.

The benefits of advanced-level courses outweigh the drawbacks. Some of the advantages are more far-reaching than simply making your child more appealing to prospective colleges. Some high schools award extra credit to students who take AP courses. Also, many people believe that students who take rigorous high school classes—such as honors and AP courses—are better prepared to manage the workload they'll face in college, more likely to receive higher grades, and less likely to drop out than their peers.

The International Baccalaureate Program

The International Baccalaureate Organization's (IB) Diploma Programme, created in 1968, is a comprehensive and challenging preuniversity course that demands the best from motivated students and teachers. This sophisticated 2-year curriculum covers a wide range of academic subjects and has stood the test of time for more than 500,000 students in 119 countries since 1968. The world's leading universities welcome IB graduates because the rigor of the curriculum is well-known. Diploma candidates are required to undertake original research and write an extended essay of about 4,000 words. This project offers the opportunity to investigate a topic of special interest and acquaints students with the kind of independent research and writing skills expected at a university. Students who graduate from the program may earn college credit or advanced standing at many colleges or universities. The program has earned a reputation for rigorous assessment, giving IB diploma holders access to the world's leading universities. The organization has shown, over the course of 30 years, that its students are well-prepared for university work (Boyd, 1999). The IB lists college recognition policies and gives other information on its Web site (http://www.ibo.org).

The IB program also includes a primary middle school curriculum. The Middle Years Programme for students ages 11–16 consists of a core curriculum program in English, mathematics, science, foreign language, and social studies. It is intended to be a 5-year program, following on the heels of the IB Primary Years Programme.

Early Entrance to College

Some gifted adolescents have a difficult time with the organizational patterns and the ordinary pace of secondary school education, even while taking advanced courses. Impatient with a secondary school system and an academic structure that does not meet their needs, they accelerate their courses to leave high school early. Most colleges will take students who have finished 3 years of high school. However, many colleges are reluctant to accept younger students without evidence of emotional maturity. Early entrance programs (discussed further in Appendix A of this guide) can provide a combined high school and college curriculum that may be more appropriate for extraordinarily gifted young people. In such programs, these students may, for the first time, find true peers, or others who share their passion for learning.

Students who want to be radically accelerated (that is, accelerated more than one grade) need to think about early entrance in terms of what they will miss if they skip 2 or more years of high school. This needs to be a family decision, in part because families will incur college expenses before they are ready. There are fewer scholarships available to underage students than there are for students who enter "on time." However, there are advantages, as well (Robinson & Davidson Institute, 2005). Students who love learning, feel a hunger to acquire a deeper understanding of the world, and enjoy communicating in writing may find a more compatible fit in college. Students who expect a long educational path to a career may want to get an early start. For example, students who know they will need multiple degrees (e.g., both an M.D. and a Ph.D.) can expect to attend school for many years. For profoundly gifted students, early entrance may not be the solution to every problem, but it may be a better fit than high school.

The disadvantages of early entrance should be recognized and discussed. If high school sports, music, journalism, or any other high school activity that is important to a student will be hard to give up, then high school may be a better fit, at least for a while. Young students might find that they are the youngest on campus, and need to stay at home while attending college. These students may miss out on some of the most significant college experiences and bonding that takes place when students live together away from home. The various options and alternatives (e.g., taking online courses, competitions, AP or IB classes) should be discussed with the entire family, for when a young student attends college, the entire family feels the impact (Robinson & Davidson Institute, 2005). Talking to other students who have chosen early entrance and reading guidebooks and other information on the topic may help students and families to think through the options.

Developing a Plan

Every gifted student should be strongly encouraged by the end of eighth grade to develop a 4-year academic plan that includes academic courses required for graduation and courses desired for college planning. The plan should also include how a student will manage his time, showing the hours he will spend in academic high school classes, those he will spend in extracurricular activities, those needed for homework, and the hours needed for family activities, rest, and relaxation. When time is planned carefully, and when plans are monitored and reviewed annually, students learn how to manage their time effectively and how to set priorities.

Effective Work/Study Skills and Time Management

Some kids find it especially difficult to manage their time. They start a project and lose track of time. They are so intensely focused that they honestly don't hear you when you call them to dinner for the third time. When a child is so interested and stimulated by the world, school projects and afterschool programs can easily become overwhelming. Highly motivated minds often strive for perfectionism and idealism, leading many gifted kids to overcommit themselves and even feel burned out. You are your child's best resource, so become a time management expert now, and launch a smooth back-to-school routine. Keep track of what works and what doesn't, so you can launch into a successful routine every year until your children go to college or

71

leave home. Managing time well is the most significant way in which effective and ineffective students differ from one another (Robinson & Davidson Institute, 2005)

Many students are able to breeze though school, taking on new classes and activities with barely a thought. School is relatively easy for them until seventh grade (or even later than that). There has been no need for these students to learn to study effectively or manage their time wisely. These students often underestimate how much time will be needed to do homework in a demanding program. When truly challenged late in high school or in college, they may discover that they do not have the skills needed to organize, study, and produce high-quality work. By the time they graduate from high school, students should have some idea as to how to study in different ways for different academic subjects and different types of assessments.

Helping adolescents manage their time depends in large part on their thinking style. Some students are systematic; they keep neat notebooks and like to organize. Their desks and lockers are neat, and have a place for everything, with similar items grouped together. They usually take tests well, especially when these tests have multiple-choice questions. Other students are more creative and organize differently. They might keep everything on their bedroom floor, but they know exactly where something is when they need it. They don't test particularly well, but they tend to write wonderful essays. The following sections (meant for student use) will provide a jumping off point for learning to effectively and proactively manage one's time.

One way to manage your time is to set up a time management chart, delegating certain amounts of your time each week to certain activities, like school, sleep, and practice. At the beginning of the school year, try to break down your time each week according to each activity. Record those breakdowns on a chart like the one on page 73–74. Each time you want to add an activity, or if you find your activities are taking up more or less time than you set aside, go back to the chart and readjust your figures. You can trade out activities (such as talking on the phone or surfing the

Time Management Chart for Students

The following chart shows the way you spend your time during an average week on various activities. If it does not include everything you do, be sure to add in activities or you won't get a realistic picture of your time. Estimate the amount of time spent on each item. Once you have this amount, multiply it by the number indicated (some questions do not require multiplication). This will give you the total time spent on the activity in 1 week. After each item's weekly time has been calculated, add all of these times together for the grand total. Subtract this from 168, the total possible hours per week. The remaining hours are the hours you have allowed yourself to study. If you have zero hours to study, go back and see what you can cut down or eliminate.

1. Number of hours of sleep each night: _____ X 7 = _____

2. Number of grooming hours per day: _____ X 7 = _____

3. Number of hours for meals/snacks per day—include preparation time:

   _____ X 7 = _____

4. Total travel time to and from school on weekdays:

   _____ X 5 = _____

5. Number of hours per week for regularly scheduled functions (music lessons, sports, family chores, religious school, babysitting, etc.):

   _____

6. Number of hours per week for scheduled extracurricular activities: _____

7. Number of hours per day for chores, errands, etc.:

   _____ X 7 = _____

73

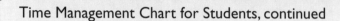

Time Management Chart for Students, continued

8. Number of hours spent in school per day:

   _____ X 5 = _____

9. Number of average hours per week socializing on the phone or with friends: _____

   Now add up the totals: _____

   Subtract the above number from 168, the number of hours in a week:

   168 − _____ = _____

Internet) for others (such as a once-in-a-lifetime concert or attending your school's football games every other week during the fall). When you have major school projects or assignments, predict how long the assignment will take by breaking it down into steps—allotting specific amounts of time for specific tasks (i.e., 2 hours to write the first draft, an hour for revisions, etc.). Then, determine if you need to schedule more time for homework each week until the project is completed. You may want to consider setting aside a particular time to work on organizing your chart each week or month. Keeping an up-to-date, thorough time management chart will help you make the most of your time, enjoy the activities you want to take part in, and ensure that your responsibilities, like finishing your homework or writing those college essays, get done.

Another way to think about time management is to create pictures. This is good for students who are visual learners. Make a time chart that looks like a favorite food or topic. For example, picture a multilayered hamburger (see Figure

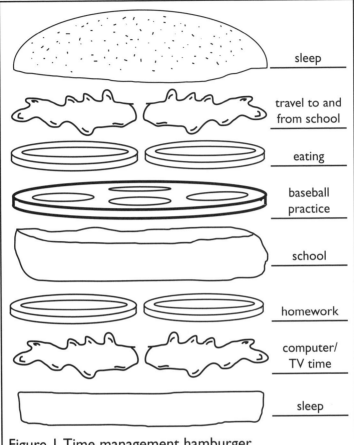

sleep

travel to and from school

eating

baseball practice

school

homework

computer/ TV time

sleep

Figure 1. Time management hamburger

Note. Adapted from "Time Management for Gifted Kids," by the Council for Exceptional Children Family Education Network, 2005, http://school.familyeducation.com/organization/gifted-education/38344.html. Copyright ©2005 by the Council for Exceptional Children. Used with permission.

1). The meat is at the center. What does the meat represent? School? Home? Let's say that the meat represents school or learning. In a 24-hour day, how much lettuce, cheese, or ketchup will you need? Is cheese the homework? Is the sauce your free time? Any image will work as long as it has tiers or pieces that are a different size from one another. This kind of time management may make a lot more sense than a time chart with arbitrary divisions.

Decision-Making Skills

There are some adolescents who make decisions easily and intuitively know how to weigh risks. Decision making is second nature to these adolescents, but needs to be taught to others who may not be able to anticipate outcomes. Your child needs to know how to evaluate choices and alternative solutions, make judgments, and test solutions if she is going to make decisions that are in her best interests. Where college planning is concerned, you can play a large part in helping your child learn to evaluate her decisions. Highly creative students may need to be taught evaluation skills while they are looking at the differences between colleges. These students receive a lot of mail from colleges. If they can't separate what information is useful from what isn't, they might wind up keeping everything and then finding nothing when they need it.

It is especially important to teach decision-making skills to multipotential adolescents who perform well in all academic areas and are involved in a variety of extracurricular activities. Eventually, they will need to choose areas of concentration and set priorities. Decision-making skills are equally important for students who are highly sensitive to expectations of others, particularly when those expectations conflict with self-fulfillment. Students also need to learn that choosing *not* to decide is a choice that may determine a person's future. They need to be able to connect outcomes with the decisions they make.

A skillful decision maker follows these steps when making good decisions:

- Know something about yourself.
- Recognize and define the decision to be made (what school courses to take, how to select a college academic major, what colleges or universities to consider).
- Assess and evaluate the information you have. Decide what facts and ideas are missing.
- Generate strategies to acquire additional information.
- Gather additional information, facts, and ideas related to the goal.

- Assess the advantages, disadvantages, and consequences (risks and costs) of each alternative by asking the following questions:
  - Will I be satisfied with this choice?
  - Will I be happy with this choice?
  - Will others (parents) approve of this choice?
  - How will I feel about this choice in 6 months? in 1 year? in 5 years?

- Make a choice. Write it down. State it aloud. Does it feel right? If the answer is no, repeat the process using another choice.
- Develop a plan or strategy to obtain the desired goal.
- Review the outcome. If it doesn't make sense, begin again. Make sure that the process itself (i.e., following the steps precisely) doesn't get in the way of reaching a decision.
- Distinguish between decisions and outcomes. (Good decisions can have poor outcomes, and vice versa.)

First, try this process when selecting a movie or purchasing music. Did it work? Try to apply this process to college planning.

Your Child's Guidance Counselor

Parents, you should establish and maintain a positive working relationship with your child's guidance counselor in middle school, and particularly in high school. This valuable professional can provide information about curricula, accelerated courses, enrichment classes, summer opportunities, and various educational options. Because your child's guidance counselor is familiar with your school and home communities, his or her perspective and expertise will prove invaluable when making plans for secondary and undergraduate study. In addition to selecting appropriate, challenging courses, the counselor can recommend programs and resources that will nurture your child's gifts and talents.

77

Your child's counselor can be your child's best friend and adviser. However, almost 60% of eighth-grade students in the nation go to high school without having discussed the selection of their courses with a school counselor (Frome & Dunham, 2002). When asked how frequently they met with their guidance counselors, most of the students interviewed for this book responded by saying "Not enough; sometimes once a year, sometimes two or three times."

The average counselor is responsible for anywhere between 500 and 1,000 students, many of whom are experiencing serious personal problems. The gifted students interviewed for this book said that their guidance counselors are doing the best they can, but because they must respond to so many needs, the job seems impossible. It is not surprising, therefore, that our gifted children are reluctant to use a counselor's time to discuss problems or future plans. Some feel their concerns are not nearly as critical as those experienced by other students and, because they are logical people, they can figure out solutions by themselves. Unfortunately, they tend to believe the myth that gifted students can make it on their own.

This year, there are high school seniors all over the U.S. receiving acceptance letters from colleges of their choice and deciding where to enroll in the fall. There are also many high school seniors whose academic achievement places them in the top tiers of the nation, but who will not enroll in college after high school because they are from poor families. What is ironic, according to a recent study by sociologists at Johns Hopkins University, is that this "talent loss" among students from low-income environments often has relatively little to do with their families' financial wherewithal. Instead, it often occurs because these students never receive practical advice on applying to college from their high school guidance counselors or other adults (Plank & Jordan, 2001). They didn't plan for college well. Many didn't seriously start to look into college until the second semester of their senior year. Often, they hadn't taken the ACTs, SATs or other achievement tests when they needed to, or they had made poor choices in course selections. A large number didn't know about the availability of financial aid and scholarships and assumed that they couldn't afford college.

As a parent, it is your responsibility to make sure that your child sees a guidance counselor to discuss his or her choice of courses and to develop a 4-year plan. If possible, you should also attend that meeting. And, make sure your child sees the counselor every year, so that by the time the counselor has to write a college recommendation, the counselor will know your teen well enough to describe in detail why he or she will be successful in college. (This book includes a form [in Chapter 5] that may help your counselor write a helpful recommendation letter.)

Career Exploration

Nothing is so simple for me that I can do a perfect job without effort, but nothing is so hard that I cannot do it. This is why I find it so difficult to decide my place in the future.

—A gifted student

How does math translate into a career if you don't want to teach math? What kind of preparation do you need for a career as a performing artist or an architect? Why learn history when you know you will never work in a museum or teach history? These are some of the questions adolescents ask. The problems encountered by some students are illustrated by the response to an interview with a 22-year-old multitalented graduate of a prestigious university, who said, "School taught me to make rational choices, but how does a rational mind navigate when options are infinite and nebulous? I need some time to tune my instincts. I need some experiences."

Mentors or internships can fill some of the need for experience. For example, Ashley decided during ninth grade that she wanted to become a talk show host someday. She applied for and was awarded an internship at a local television channel, and spent time there after school for the next few months. During her internship, she saw the less glamorous aspects of being a talk show host and talked to professionals about their schooling. At the end of her internship, she decided that she preferred advertising, and ultimately was highly successful in that field.

It is common to attribute extraordinary powers to gifted students who are preparing for the world of work. Contrary to popular thinking, however, they need special help to prepare for that world, in part because of their characteristics and in part because an occupation often becomes lifelong career development for gifted students. Gifted students need more, not less, information and assistance with career planning, because some have more options and alternatives than they can realistically consider and some are caught in a conflict between self-fulfillment and pleasing other people. Too often, gifted young people are expected to succeed on their own or adapt to whatever situations they happen to encounter; thus, career planning is left to chance.

Focusing on Your Future

Many colleges and universities hold all-day or longer academic and career planning activities for secondary gifted students, ages 11–16. Students are given opportunities to interact with professionals in varied fields and parents are informed about career-oriented academic planning. College faculty or professionals lead career workshops in the humanities and social sciences, art, mathematics, science, and technology. Parent sessions include topics such as college planning and finances, encouraging girls in math and science, and the social and emotional needs of gifted students.

Career exploration should help students understand the relationship between school and careers, become familiar with realistic career options, set short- and long-term goals, and plan for the future. That is why career exploration is a self-discovery process. Most adolescents don't have a clue as to what they want to do as adults. Some know what they'll do when they are young children, but those students are in the minority. Because the world is so complex, many of our gifted adolescents will be some of the first to work in their career fields.

When students are not provided with appropriate career planning information in high school, they may choose college majors or careers prematurely and arbitrarily, or delay decision making until well into adulthood. Even students who do not attend college do not settle into a career until 5 or 6 years after they graduate (Johns Hopkins University, n.d.; Plank & Jordan, 2001).

Gifted high school students take career planning seriously. However, high school teachers barely have time to cover the syllabus, and rarely engage in career guidance. Some high schools have career centers, but no adult works in the career center to help students with these decisions. In addition, gifted students tend to change majors at least once during college, and some change majors four or five times, and continue to express uncertainty about career choices later in life (Kaufmann, 1981; Simpson & Kaufmann, 1981).

Career planning based on a student's values, interests, needs, and personal cognitive style, as opposed to aptitudes and abilities, seems to be more effective than traditional methods for youngsters who are gifted. A broad approach to career awareness for gifted students should address the following issues:

- self-awareness (i.e., understanding one's personal values, interests, personality, and skills);
- understanding present and future career options;
- understanding how high school courses, college majors, and advanced degrees relate to careers;
- understanding that multiple interests can be combined into a career;
- participating in internships, mentorships, and other hands-on experiences; and
- understanding that some interests are associated with specific careers and some interests become leisure activities. Gifted adults are unlikely to find self-fulfillment through work alone.

Career Centers

Many schools consider career centers an integral part of their academic resources. Research for this book included a 2-hour interview with a career center coordinator. The interview was conducted in the career center, a room the size of an average classroom. During the interview, counselors, teachers, parents, and students came to the center, used its resources independently, and departed. Students worked on computers or ate lunch while reading. Parent volunteers arrived, entered data on computers, catalogued books, and performed other time-consuming tasks. The coordinator, occasionally interrupted by a student, parent, counselor, or teacher asking a question, outlined the practices and objectives of the center, including the following:

- A flexible 4-year plan guided all activities. Students were assigned objectives each year, including appropriate interest inventories and assessment tests. For example, ninth-grade students learned how to use the resources and how to investigate appropriate career clusters.
- Students kept a file of test results and research conclusions.
- Students discussed test results with guidance counselors and the career center coordinator during individual discussions or group counseling workshops.

A career center can make a vital difference in the quality of a career planning program. Counselors, teachers, parents, and students should push for this resource in every school, but if it's not doable, teach your son or daughter to use the career materials in the public library. What follows is a list of materials students should become familiar with. To start a "bare bones" career center, you would need the following:

- *O*net Dictionary of Occupational Titles: The Definitive Printed Reference of Occupational Information* (DOT; 2004; ISBN# 1-56370-962-7) describes nearly 1,000 jobs. The book includes current information on each job's education and training level, earnings, projected growth, number of openings, number of people employed, skills, personality type, and much more. Each thorough description includes specific tasks performed, earnings, education and training requirements, plus ratings on dozens of skills, temperaments, physical requirements, verbal and math proficiencies, and much more. It is possible to show a student the differences among such job titles as psychiatrist and psychologist, and others. There is also a code that establishes the degree of involvement with data, people, and things for each title. It is excellent as a beginning tool to show students some of what matters in occupational selection. The classification system is the basis for many other sources.

- *Occupational Outlook Handbook* (OOH; 2006; ISBN# 1-59357-248-4), published by the U.S. Department of Labor, provides more information than the DOT for the jobs that employ the most people in the United States. An expanded job description, training required, salary, related jobs, and the hiring outlook for the next 10 years, as well as an address where the student can write for free information about the occupation that interests him, are included. This source is reissued every 2 years, in hard or soft cover.

- *New Guide for Occupational Exploration: Linking Interests, Learning, and Careers* (2005; ISBN# 1-59357-180-1) is an organizational tool for setting up occupational files and cross-indexing all of your information. It contains what it calls Worker Trait Groups, a rationale for each group, and an alphabetic index to occupations, using the DOT number and the Worker Trait Group number.

- Chronicle Guidance materials (see http://www.chronicleguidance.com) are excellent, and the 3-in-1 subscription they offer gives more for the money than anything else. Included are monthly issues of occupational briefs and reprints; guidance materials; the *Four-Year College Handbook* (ISBN# 1-55631-335-7) and the *Two-Year College Handbook* (ISBN# 1-55631-334-9), which offer indexes of majors, as well as information about colleges in easy to compare chart form; a handbook to use with trade and technical schools; and a volume that gives addresses for free occupational materials for your files. The handbook for trade and technical schools varies by region: Northeast, West, and Midwest. This is an annual subscription. It takes about 4 years to collect the entire occupational library, but it is one system that begins with a subscription and then builds to include the full collection, rather than requiring patrons to pay for the whole collection up front.

- A college handbook is next on the list; you may consider using *Peterson's Four-Year Colleges* (2006; ISBN# 0-76891-749-2). Peterson's book has a chart of admissions by SAT percentile that keeps a student from assuming that medians are absolute. This book, and most other college handbooks, is published annually; it must be purchased every year.

- File folders for setting up files in three categories: postsecondary education (it is best not to file colleges and trade/technical school materials separately), occupations, and job skills.

- Additional guides, including some or all of the following:
  ○ *Fiske Guide to Colleges* (2006; ISBN# 1-40220-374-8; http://www.fiskeguide.com);
  ○ Greenes' Guides to Educational Planning (http://www.greenesguides.com);
  ○ books published by Wintergreen Orchard House (http://www.wgoh.com); and
  ○ books published by Octameron Associates (http://www.octameron.com).

Before you purchase anything, visit the Web site of the National Career Development Association (http://www.ncda.org). This Web site is filled with links to useful sites on career planning and specific career information.

Resources and Assessment Tools for Career Exploration

Aptitude tests, interest inventories, other standardized instruments, and a variety of additional resources are used by school systems, counselors, and teachers to help students learn about themselves and set short- and long-term educational and career goals. These instruments are useful because they provide a great deal of information in a minimum amount of time. Some instruments provide information at a relatively low cost. However, most aptitude tests and interest inventories must be used with caution for the following reasons:

- Some tests designed for the general public are inappropriate for gifted students, who tend to score in the 98th to 99th percentiles in all areas, because the ceiling is too low. Many gifted students score in the uppermost deciles in all scales, demonstrating a high, flat profile. These students doubt the usefulness of the tests. As one student commented after taking an aptitude test, "I can be either a mechanic or a neurosurgeon."
- Most aptitude tests cannot discriminate among high levels of performance; thus they do not reflect the relative strengths and weaknesses of gifted students.

A variety of instruments may be useful for adults who wish to provide gifted students with information about themselves to use in short- and long-term planning. This includes tools for values clarification and appropriate inventories that assess interests, personal needs, and learning styles. Values clarification encourages students to understand themselves better and to develop belief systems and behavior codes that they can later use as a foundation for some of the most important decisions of their lives. Interest inventories are designed to help students understand themselves, their possible career directions, and the educational preparation necessary for various career alternatives. Some inventories do not give gifted students sufficient information

85

about careers that have existed for only a few years; however, combined with values clarification, decision-making skills, and appropriate group and individual guidance counseling, these instruments can be helpful. Personal needs assessments help students understand the ways in which their personality characteristics integrate with careers. Learning style inventories help students understand the way they prefer to learn.

The following instruments are appropriate for gifted students. Many of them are available in a computerized version.

- **The Harrington-O'Shea Career Decision-Making System** developed by American Guidance Service (http://www.agsnet.com). The design of this tool makes it easy to administer, and it provides most students with an adequate interpretation of their preferences. However, it does not distinguish among science clusters. For example, the student whose primary interest is physical science may not produce scores indicating science as a preferred career category, if he or she rejects life science activities. The Career Decision-Making System has a variety of levels in English and Spanish.

- **The Career Occupational Preference System (COPS)**, published by Educational & Industrial Testing Service (http://www.edits.net/cops.html). COPS matches interests with certain career clusters. Because distinctions are made between different science clusters—for example, physical science, life science, and mathematical science, this test has been used successfully with gifted students.

- **Self-Directed Search (SDS; 4th ed.)** Holland (1962) developed his model by analyzing responses from National Merit finalists, which suggests that it should be relevant for use with gifted individuals. Gifted adolescents often find the Holland theory of vocational choice helpful because it generates a three-letter "Holland Code," based on inclusion in the following groups:
  ○ Realistic type: likes to work with things (e.g., tools, objects, machines, or animals)

- ○ Investigative type: tends to be curious, studious, and independent; will be successful in any area where creative problem defining or problem solving is valued
- ○ Artistic type: creative, freewheeling, tends to dislike routine
- ○ Social type: prefers activities in which the primary focus is on helping other people
- ○ Enterprising type: likes activities that permit leading or influencing other people. The most successful people in fields associated with this type are outgoing, energetic, persistent people who are committed to an idea
- ○ Conventional type: likes activities that permit organization of information in a clear and orderly way; is responsible and dependable

Students can use this tool by imagining they are at a party and people from each of the above six groups are gathered in separate locations in a room. Which group are you most attracted to? Select three groups this way and write down the first letter of each of the three groups you would prefer to spend time with. That will give you your own 3-letter code. Now, go online to the University of Missouri Career Center Web site (http://career.missouri.edu/students/explore/thecareerinterestsgame.php), and match your codes with their job possibilities by running your mouse over each group heading.

This exercise will give students a general idea of the career possibilities to think about. The exercise can also be played online at an SDS Web site (http://www.self-directed-search.com is one to try). They will give you feedback for a small fee.

87

Middle School/Intermediate School Instruments

Career planning instruments can also be used successfully with middle school students. An instrument that has proven to be helpful to middle school students thinking about future careers is the FIRO-B Scale.

The FIRO-B Scale, a personal needs inventory, is published by Consulting Psychologists Press for students in grades 8–16 and adults. This untimed inventory takes approximately 120 minutes to complete. FIRO-B stands for Fundamental Interpersonal Relations Orientation. The FIRO-B Scale is a self-reporting questionnaire designed to assess a person's need for inclusion, control, and affection in various aspects of interpersonal situations (Thorndike & Hagan, 1986). The test is generally administered to 9th and 10th grade students. However, gifted students need the information earlier, because they tend to make decisions before their agemates. The FIRO-B Scale can be used effectively with intermediate or middle school gifted students to help them become more aware of their affective needs.

Software

Technological advancement has added a new dimension to career counseling—computer-based career information and guidance systems. Although the technology is still unfolding, interviews indicate that computer-based career information and guidance systems are being used successfully with gifted students, including the DISCOVER and SIGI software programs.

DISCOVER, available from the American College Testing Program (ACT) at http://www.act.org/discover, was developed as a systematic career guidance program to assist in career development activities at the secondary school level. The package includes values and decision-making education, relating and exploring occupations, and career exploration and planning. SIGI[3] (System of Interactive Guidance and Information), published by Educational Testing Service (ETS; available at http://www.valparint.com), is based on the assumption that a person's values are the overriding factor in his or her career choice. The computer system weighs the relative strengths of 10 values (including income, level of independence, helping others, security, fields of interest, and leadership) and tests the user by considering combinations of hypothetical jobs, each of which stresses one particular value. When values conflict, the computer warns the user of the discrepancy and asks the user to reconsider. For example, if a student says, "I want to help people" and "earn $100,000 a year," the program recognizes a conflict in goals and provides alternatives.

What Parents Can Do

If your school has a career center, volunteer. If possible, set up a program that matches students with adults in careers. However, speakers should be carefully chosen for their ability to relate to adolescents. Students are generally interested in any or all of the following:

- the nature of the person's work;
- prior work experiences leading to the person's current position;
- how the person became interested in the work;
- the advantages and disadvantages, positive and negative aspects of the work;
- a typical workday;
- formal educational preparation;
- college courses the person found most valuable;
- college courses the person wishes he or she had taken;
- the long-range job opportunities in the person's field; and
- the current and potential salary range.

Talk about your work—its positive and negative aspects, its advantages and disadvantages, and future opportunities in the field. If possible, take your adolescent where you work and show him or her what you do. In addition, ask open-ended questions when your student mentions careers. (Avoid statements that inadvertently transmit expectations.) Encourage your child to explore in depth as many careers as possible, and encourage community involvement, particularly volunteer activities. Overall, keep in mind that many people change careers several times during their work life.

89

What Teachers Can Do

Teachers, you should assist students in career planning in the following ways:

- Discuss teaching and specific fields of teaching with students—including the educational requirements, advantages and disadvantages, and future opportunities.
- Encourage students to read biographies and other material about people who work in education.
- Encourage girls to explore mathematical and scientific fields.
- Encourage boys to explore the humanities and/or a liberal arts college, especially if they plan to pursue a specialized mathematical or scientific field.
- Discuss ways that your discipline is related to different careers.
- Provide opportunities for students to write critically and speak effectively about the way their careers might relate to the future.

What Counselors Can Do

Career planning is most effective when designed as a coherent 4-year program in which, by the end of 11th grade, gifted students can ask and begin to answer the following questions:

- How is school related to my personal career goals?
- How do vocational assessments and inventories relate to my goals?
- What specific steps can I take to explore and investigate fields that appear to be appropriate for me?
- What type of research will give me answers to questions I ask?
- How can I get an apprenticeship, internship, or mentor?
- What types of work activities do I prefer?
- What types of work situations do I like?
- What careers do I want to avoid? Why?

Learning About Colleges: What Do They Have That I Want?

There are more than 3,500 colleges in the United States. Some are more selective than others. Some are "name brand" colleges, while some of the nation's best colleges are not well-known institutions. Eventually your teen should make a list of about 20 schools that look like a potential match, and over time, narrow the list to about 5–8 colleges. Your teen can begin by writing down what she thinks is most important in a school. For example, some students do not like flying and should avoid applying to colleges that require flying to get home. Or, students who hate snow should avoid cities where it snows from October to May. In addition, students who want to join a fraternity or sorority in college should look for universities with a strong Greek system already in place.

The final group should include at least one school where your son or daughter is sure of acceptance (a safety school), one school where admissions criteria are slightly beyond the adolescent's credentials (a long shot), and three or four colleges where admissions criteria match the student's credentials (i.e., the required SAT or ACT score, GPA, class rank, etc.). Your family will need to visit all of the schools in the final group, so plan ahead and consult the section of this chapter on visiting colleges. Consult college planning reference guides for academic admissions criteria for the schools that interest

Common Pitfalls for Students to Avoid

"I'm applying to college X because all my friends are/are not going there."

"There's only one college that's right for me."

"All colleges are the same, so why bother with all this work?"

"I'm going to college X because my father/mother/sister/brother went there (or wants me to go there)."

"College X is too expensive for me."

"I'm not applying there because I'll be rejected." (This does not mean you should avoid applying to one "long-shot" school.)

"If the one college I want doesn't want me, I'll be unhappy for the next 4 years."

your teen. Although finances will enter the picture at some point, keep in mind that many private schools award some level of tuition assistance to most of their students. The longer a student attends a school and is academically successful there, the more scholarship opportunities will be available to him or her.

There is a huge difference between high school and college, particularly the level of independence and personal freedom. High school is mandatory and free; college is voluntary and expensive. In high school, students do not have complete control over the way they spend their time. In college, they are free to set their own schedules. High school teachers may approach the student who is having academic problems. College faculty members are less likely to approach students, although they are likely to be helpful and friendly when students seek assistance. Some students never needed to study during high school. College is probably the end of that, as studying for several hours outside of class for

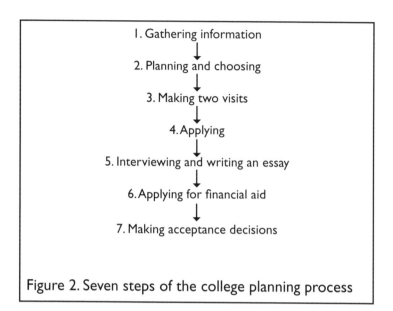

1. Gathering information

2. Planning and choosing

3. Making two visits

4. Applying

5. Interviewing and writing an essay

6. Applying for financial aid

7. Making acceptance decisions

Figure 2. Seven steps of the college planning process

each hour spent in class or lab is likely to occur in college. Students who disliked high school because of its structure may be much happier in college. Students who are happier when a structure is imposed may have a bumpy transitional path during their freshman year.

Learning about colleges involves seven steps (see Figure 2): (1) gathering information, (2) planning and choosing, (3) making two visits, (4) applying, (5) interviewing and writing an essay, (6) applying for financial aid, and (7) making acceptance decisions. Parents, the rest of this chapter is intended to be used by students, but you can gain a lot of information about the college planning process from it, as well.

Step 1: Gathering Information

Step 1 of the college search process involves collecting general information by visiting Web sites, reading guidebooks and using multimedia resources, talking with people (asking questions), and visiting colleges. From the very beginning of your college search, the Internet can be a valuable tool. A good place to start is with Web sites that provide databases of colleges such as the College Board, Peterson's, and others listed in Appendix B of this book. Depending on the site, you may be able to type in the geographical area, size, setting, major(s), and other characteristics that interest you. You'll then see a list of colleges that match your preferences. These comparative sites are a great way to generate a long list of colleges to research further. You might find colleges you haven't even thought of. Some comparative sites only include the colleges that pay for the privilege of being listed, so you could miss some good options if you rely on only one site. You'll find that some comparative sites have more information than others about individual colleges. Also, keep in mind that a comparative site may not have the most up-to-date information on deadlines and other time-sensitive material. For that, it's best to check the colleges' Web sites directly.

What Students Can Do to Learn About Colleges

Your guidance counselor and parents can help you learn about yourself and develop a list of things you consider important when selecting colleges. One of the first things you can do is close your eyes and visualize yourself walking toward a campus building. What you see may be used to start looking for a college. Did you see yourself walking down a busy street toward your dorm? Or, did you see yourself walking toward classes with friends on a green, carpet-like campus lawn? Write down everything you see, down to the smallest detail, because later the details will become more important.

You can do the following to learn about colleges and college offerings:

- Become familiar with different types of college guides and multimedia resources.
- Ask questions. Talk to college students, graduates, and college representatives.
- Visit a wide range of colleges.

College Guidebooks and Multimedia Resources

There are two types of college guides: *objective guides* that provide information from a database such as number of students or average SATs, and *subjective guides* that provide information based on opinion, such as "10 hottest schools."

Objective Guides. Objective guides provide categorical and statistical data on every 2- and/or 4-year college and university in the United States, Canada, and other countries. They list colleges and universities alphabetically or by state; most also list the telephone number for the Office of Admissions. The following guides offer data-based information. Because they are updated every year, the ISBN numbers and years have not been listed for these resources; however, a current copy of each can easily be found at your local bookstore or an online bookseller.

- *Profiles of American Colleges* by Barron's.
- *Fiske Guide to Colleges* by Edward Fiske.
- *Peterson's Four-Year Colleges* by Thomson Peterson's.
- *The College Board College Handbook* by the College Board.
- *America's Best Value Colleges,* by Eric Owens, Tom Meltzer, and the staff of the Princeton Review.

In addition, you may want to check out the Princeton Review's package of guides, which includes the *Complete Book of Colleges* and *The Best 361 Colleges* (Meltzer et al., 2006). To compile *The Best 361 Colleges,* the editors asked more than 110,000 college students what their schools were really like. The "Best Party School" ranking list gets a lot of attention, but it is just one small part of this guide. Check out which schools were most likely to have "Dorms Like Dungeons," and other interesting student-based opinions (Meltzer et al.). This package combines both objective and subjective guides that complement each other nicely.

Objective guides provide data-based college profiles that are written by the colleges and, hence, may be designed to cast each college in a favorable light. However, this fact does not negate their usefulness. Objective college guides contain similar information but differ in several ways:

95

- Some objective guides have specific orientations; for example, a section on careers. The section may be useful, but it may not be appropriate for every gifted student.
- Some objective guides are more thorough in breadth, depth, and scope of coverage.
- Some objective guides include worksheets that allow students to map the college selection process; this is particularly useful for some students.
- Some objective guides are revised annually and contain up-to-date information on the cost of tuition, room, and board.
- A companion index of majors accompanies some objective guides. This index provides information for students who know what they want to study, but not where to study it. The index is particularly helpful to students who want to combine academic majors (e.g., physics and philosophy) or major in an area that is relatively uncommon (e.g., a specialized microbiological science).

The statistical information provided by objective guides can be used in different ways. For example, most college profiles list the number of undergraduate students enrolled. When you visit a college, investigate the relationship between college size and the size of an average freshman class. You may find that some classes are gigantic, but the college offers supplemental freshman seminars. The size of the student body will affect your opportunities and experiences, including the range of academic majors offered and extracurricular possibilities. When considering size, look beyond the raw number of students who attend the school to the size of the department that interests you. Is the faculty in this department accessible to the students?

Guides also list admissions standards, including the school's basis for selection and the average SAT and/or ACT scores of entering freshmen. The average scores are not adjusted to reflect students who leave the school prior to graduation. You can use the graphic breakdown of each institution's SAT/ACT scores to determine how comfortable you will be academically. The SAT and ACT assessments have undergone radical changes; both added a writing require-ment and made some adjustments in the multiple-choice questions. You may not be able to compare all your scores to those of students currently enrolled in the college or univer-sity. However, you might be able to compare just your verbal and math scores. Based on this information, if your scores fall in the top or middle of the range, you will probably be comfortable at this school. If your scores fall in the bottom third, prepare yourself for rigorous coursework and an aca-demic challenge.

Additional information can be obtained when you visit a college. Ask about the SAT/ACT scores of students who chose to enroll in the academic major you are consider-ing. Again, your compiled score can't be compared, but you should be able to get an idea of how your math and verbal scores compare with those of students who have completed that academic major successfully. Bear in mind, however, that SAT/ACT scores of students who have completed an academ-ic major are only one way of estimating whether or not you will be comfortable with a school's academic expectations, and it will take colleges several years before they know how to evaluate the new 2400-point SAT or the revised ACT.

Subjective Guides. Subjective guides are similar to ob-jective guides, but limit the colleges discussed to specific groups, or focus on specific topics. Unlike many objective guides, these books are updated often, but not necessarily every year. Therefore, an ISBN number has been included to help you find each guide. Subjective guides include the following books:

- *Choosing the Right College: The Whole Truth About America's Top Schools* (2005; ISBN# 1-93223-634-1) by the Intercollegiate Studies Institute.
- *The Ultimate College Guide* (2005; ISBN# 1-40220-596-1) by *U.S. News & World Report.*
- *The Insider's Guide to the Colleges* (2005; ISBN# 0-31234-157-1) by the Yale Daily News.
- *Colleges That Change Lives: 40 Schools You Should Know About Even If You're Not a Straight-A Student* (2000; ISBN# 0-14029-616-6) by Loren Pope.

- *Looking Beyond the Ivy League: Finding the College That's Right for You* (1996; ISBN# 0-14023-952-9) by Loren Pope.
- *Cool Colleges: For the Hyper-Intelligent, Self-Directed, Late Blooming, and Just Plain Different* (2000; ISBN# 1-58008-150-9) by Donald Asher.
- *The Unofficial, Unbiased Guide to the 331 Most Interesting Colleges* (2004; ISBN# 0-74325-199-7) by Kaplan Inc.

Objective and subjective guides are used differently. In effect, subjective guides supplement objective guides. Keep in mind the following:
- Some subjective guides may not specify criteria used to rank colleges. Descriptions may in fact be one person's biased opinion, formulated during a brief, one-time visit.
- Some subjective guides rank academic departments in selected colleges; however, they may not state the criteria they have used to do so. The information may be valuable when verified during a college visit, particularly if you arrange an interview with a faculty member.
- Many college rankings change from year to year. For example, a college that was ranked No. 2 one year could drop to No. 8 the next year, or a school that was in the second tier could jump up to a top-20 category. The school might not have changed; however, the formula used for ranking colleges might have been revised. If two different magazines rank colleges differently (e.g., one uses the number of acceptances divided by the number of applications, and the other uses the yield, or the number of enrollments divided by the number of acceptances), the two different methods will produce different rankings.
- Some subjective guides only discuss student life or a specific aspect of campus lifestyle, so make sure you use a more comprehensive guide, as well.
- Some books focus on topics such as the campus visit, the application, and the essay. They may be useful, but they differ in their quality of advice.

Objective guides may be pallid, but they are often more useful than colorful subjective guides. For example, one guide may note that a school's graduate students do not teach undergraduate courses, while another may state that the university population is divided into several social cliques. Anecdotal information may be entertaining, but it also may be biased or misleading. If you want to find out how many students in a particular school graduate with a business degree (statistical information), consult an objective guide. If you want to find out about the social scene at a particular school, consult a responsible subjective guide, preferably one that collects information through questionnaires distributed to enrolled college students. Bear in mind that the social scene at every college varies from year to year and that some descriptions have been written by students who graduated prior to the book's publication date. If you are using an online guide, make sure it's the most recent version.

Admissions guides like *Harvard Schmarvard: Getting Beyond the Ivy League to the College That Is Best for You* (2003; ISBN# 0-76153-695-7) by Jay Mathews (a Harvard graduate), don't fit in either objective or subjective categories, and can be equally useful. *Harvard Schmarvard* rebuts the perception that image is everything when it comes to college and emphasizes this simple fact: What you will be measured by in life is your talent and energy, not your college's name.

Additional Resources

View books, published by most colleges and universities, are generally the first written information students receive from colleges. They are glossy publications designed to promote the college's physical appearance and campus facilities. Larger schools with many resources may emphasize technological equipment. Smaller schools with fewer resources might emphasize a homey atmosphere. View books provide superficial information that should be confirmed during a campus visit.

College Web sites, usually a student's first point of contact with a college, may take students on a narrated, picturesque visit, presenting an idyllic physical setting with students studying under a tree on a lovely spring day. Keep in mind that this idyllic scene may occur for a short period each year. You may want to visit a campus when the weather is pleasant and, again, when the weather presents inconveniences such as heavy rain or snow.

To make the most of a college's Web site, try these strategies.

- Look at the home pages of individual faculty members in majors that interest you—some post detailed syllabi of their classes, descriptions of their research interests, and e-mail addresses. If you have a specific question or two about a major, try sending a faculty member a short, polite e-mail introducing yourself and asking your questions (don't ask anything you can find out in the college catalog, though).
- Read the pages for prospective students thoroughly. They will give you basic information about the college, as well as some sense of the mission and priorities of the college.
- Visit the home pages of student organizations—you can check out the schedule for the various clubs and groups or see what resolutions student government passed during the semester.
- Look for the home pages put up by current students at the college. If students list their e-mail addresses, send short e-mail messages to a few of them, asking questions about their college experiences. Try to look at a good sampling of student pages.
- Find the alumni association pages—what are alumni of the college doing now? What is the college doing for its alumni?

Computerized databases offer another way to learn about colleges. The software is easy to use and offers fast, easy access to information. The more sophisticated programs are interactive, menu-driven, and offer a college selection service, financial aid information, and career exploration. They also offer a "why not?" option that tells users why certain colleges or career choices were not included. The scholarship search allows users to match individual characteristics, such as ethnic and multicultural backgrounds or special talents, with sources of aid, such as national and state grants and public and private scholarships.

Every college and university publishes a *catalog* describing the institution and the courses it offers. Some colleges charge a fee for the catalog unless you download it from their Web site. If you are interested in a school, reading the course catalog is useful. College catalogs can help you assess a school's distribution requirements, the kinds of courses taught, and the sizes of various academic departments. This will help you decide whether or not a particular college will meet your academic and career needs. Bear in mind that although one particular course may sound interesting, that course may not be taught each semester and may even be dropped by the time you enroll. If you are interested in specific courses, ask about them when you visit a campus. You can request information from colleges using the sample request letter in Figure 3.

Another way you can learn about colleges and universities is to *ask questions*. Take advantage of opportunities to obtain different types of information by asking questions of college representatives, college students, teachers, and others who can provide firsthand knowledge. If you know what you want to study, research reputations of academic departments by talking to people in the fields that interest you. Consider, compare, and evaluate information you receive. If you're undecided, relax and pick an academically balanced institution that offers a range of majors and programs. Most colleges offer counseling to help you find a focus.

College representatives can answer the following questions:

101

- What makes your college different from all other colleges?
- How does the college evaluate applicants? What weight is given to objective/numerical information (GPA, class rank, standardized test scores) versus subjective infor-

Director of Admissions
College of Your Choice
Address

To Whom It May Concern:

I am a student at _____ High School in (city and state). I plan
to graduate in (month) of 20____. Please send me a copy of your
latest college catalog and an application form. I also would like to
receive forms for all types of financial aid. I am considering major-
ing in _____, am also interested in _____, and would appreciate any information about these concentrations.

Thank you very much for your assistance. I look forward to hear-
ing from you soon.

Sincerely,
Your Name

**Figure 3. Sample request for written information from
a college**

mation (presentation of extracurricular activities, rec-
ommendations, the essay, and the interview)?
- How does the school evaluate SAT or ACT scores?
- Does the college require students to take specific cours-
  es or enroll in courses to fulfill certain requirements (i.e.,
  distribution requirements/core curriculum)?
- Do students have the same adviser every year?
- How does the college welcome each freshman class?
  What procedures exist for orientation, advising, and
  registration? Can I register for classes by computer?
- How does the college assist students with career plan-
  ning?
- Is the admissions process "need blind?" Are merit-based
  scholarships available?

College students can answer the following questions:
- What do you like and dislike about the location?

- Why did you select that college? How often do you go home and is it easy to get home?
- What do you wish you had known before selecting this school?
- What is campus life like? What are the "hot topics"?
- When you started college, what differences did you notice between high school and college?
- What is your average day like?
- How do you live? What kind of living arrangements does the college offer, and is housing guaranteed to anyone who wants to live on campus? What are the advantages and disadvantages of living on and off campus?
- What are classes like? Lecture halls with a huge number of students or smaller classrooms?
- Who teaches most of your classes? Professors or graduate students?
- Where do students study? Are the dorms quiet enough to study in your room?
- What kinds of relationships exist between students and faculty, and between the college and the town or city where it is located?
- What provisions are made for student's physical and mental health, safety, and security?
- Does the school help you plan a career? If so, how?

When you gather information, be sure to consider the different types of colleges and universities:
- *Small liberal arts colleges*: Likely to have smaller classes and no graduate students, but they may not have the programs of study that interest you.
- *Large private universities*: Often highly selective with a wide range of programs. A small, but growing, trend at larger universities offers students the best of both worlds: Residential colleges, a long-held tradition at some Ivy League schools, provide students with smaller communities within large universities.
- *State universities:* These often have open admission and must accept applicants from their state until a cut-off date.

103

- *Women's colleges*: Most are now coeducational, but the majority of their students are women. Their faculty also is made up primarily of women. Many prominent women claim a women's college as their alma mater.
- *Technical universities*: May emphasize computer science, math, and science. The word *technical* is part of their name (e.g., California Institute of Technology [Cal Tech] or Virginia Polytechnic Institute and State University [Virginia Tech]).
- *Comprehensive mid-size schools*: A middle ground, larger than small liberal arts schools, but smaller than private universities or state schools. Usually, these schools do not have graduate students or teaching assistants.

In addition to finding out what type of college you're applying to, you should also look for information about its admissions options. Different colleges and universities have different types of admissions options, including early decision (ED), early action (EA), and single choice early action (SCEA).

Early decision is the application process in which students make a commitment to a first-choice institution where, if admitted, they definitely will enroll. Early action is the application process in which students submit an application to an institution of preference and receive a decision well in advance of the institution's regular response rate. Single choice early action, also referred to as nonbinding early decision, can best be described as a midpoint between early decision and early action (NACAC, 2001, 2004b). Similar to ED, if a student applies to an SCEA college, the student is prohibited from applying either ED or EA to other colleges, but may apply regular admission anywhere else. Unlike ED and similar to EA, students are not bound to attend the SCEA college if they are accepted.

Whether any of these policies offers the student an advantage depends on the year. Some years a college will offer the early decision admission option to quite a few applicants, and other years they do not offer early admission to any applicants. The colleges are inconsistent on these admissions policies, so it's best to ask.

Organizing Information

If you have taken the PSATs, SATs, ACTs, or any other standardized test, you may receive information from colleges sometime in the near future. The volume and variety of information you receive can be confusing if you do not organize it in some way. In general, your life will be calmer if you figure out a system. Any method will do, even if it seems haphazard. Your particular method is not important, as long as you are organized, your system is consistent, and you understand what you are doing. For example, you can construct a chart, set up a color-coded file, develop a computer database, or use any other system that will work for you. You can start with three cartons, labeled yes, no way, and maybe.

Step 2: Planning and Choosing

During 11th grade, college-bound adolescents should have enough information to be able to plan and choose; that is, develop a list of 10 to 20 colleges based on personal criteria (what you know about yourself, your skills, and interests). (If you want to combine the last year of high school with one year of college, this process will need to be accelerated by at least a year.) Students, be sure the list includes schools where you *might* be accepted, schools where you will *probably* be accepted, and schools where you *know* you will be accepted. Your decision should be based on what you know about yourself and your values, interests, personal needs, and goals; what you learn about colleges and college offerings; and an understanding of how colleges evaluate applicants. This is not an easy task, in part because your interests, needs, and goals may change and in part because college admission standards change each year.

Once you have a preliminary list of colleges that interest you, the Internet can be helpful in researching each college further. The primary ways to research colleges online are through the individual college Web sites and through e-mail

105

contact. Most people just type the college's name into the browser box or into Google's™ search box. Once you get to the school's Web site, plan on spending some time investigating. You can find all the basics—selectivity, size, majors, setting, etc.—in addition to some clues as to what everyday life on campus is like. When you start looking at college Web sites, you will find two types of information: the official information you can get from the admissions office and the college catalog and the unofficial information you get when you read the student newspaper or contact current students. Both are valuable. Keep in mind that marketing firms have developed the official pages in order to sell you something—the school.

At this point in the college planning process, you need a way of organizing the information you have gathered so you can make some choices. Rank ordering the criteria that are important to you is a way to get started. Figure 4 will help you look at each school using the same criteria. If a criterion is not important, skip it and go on to the next.

Good decisions require good decision-making skills and good information. Two categories of good information are required:

- *Information about yourself.* Think about your interests and the experiences you have had that you really enjoyed. Let your imagination run wild and picture yourself at work. What kinds of people do you like to spend time with? Information about yourself will permit you to list the characteristics you want in a college. These should include some of the following: the college's location, type, type by sex, size, social life, academic environment, campus environment, religious affiliation, student activities, programs offered, special programs, caliber of students, cost, athletics, financial aid, housing, school calendar, and other factors.
- *Information about the world of choices.* This should include academic experiences and interests. The stronger your academic preparation, the broader your range of options. Next, make a rank-ordered list of your extracurricular experiences and interests. Eventually, your

Here are some criteria you may want to use when selecting a range of colleges. First, go through the list to determine which criteria are important to you. (Your choices might change as you learn more about schools.) Then, as you investigate colleges, fill in the names of several in the top row. Rate each characteristic on a scale of 1 to 5, based on its importance to you. Then, use your rankings to help you make a decision about which colleges you'd like to apply to.

When you select colleges, bear in mind that your list should include at least one safety school, one long shot, and several schools whose selection criteria match your qualifications.

Scale 1–5 (Poor to Excellent)

Characteristics	School A:	School B:	School C:	School D:
Size				
Location				
Cost				
Type				
Social Life				
Academic Atmosphere				
Campus Environment				
Religious Affiliation				
Student Activities				
Programs Offered				
Special Programs				
Campus Lifestyle				
Caliber of Students				
Athletics				
Financial Aid				
Housing				
Faculty				
Calendar				
Prestige				
Special Services				
Distribution Requirements				
Selectivity				
Other				

Figure 4. Determining criteria

choices will reflect your personal values, attitudes, aptitudes, interests, goals, and finances. Information about
your choices comes from several sources, including your
counselor, college fairs, and various media-related resources. Start with your guidance office. Become familiar with the college guides, multimedia resources, and
videotapes in your counselor's office. Collect literature
from college fairs. Obtain literature from your top 15 to
20 choices.

Planning and choosing involves analyzing and evaluating information you have obtained from people, written material, and Web sites. Visiting a school is the primary way to
confirm what you have discovered and separate fact from
fiction. By the middle of 12th grade, you should narrow your
list to five or six colleges by evaluating information about
college offerings and the method used by colleges to select a
freshman class. (If you are going to apply for early decision,
this process will have to take place well before the middle of
12th grade.) The final list should reflect (a) personal values,
interests, and needs; (b) the variety and range of available
college opportunities; and (c) realistic constraints, such as
cost and distance.

At this point, selectivity of the schools on the list should
also be considered, because you are looking for a match between your needs and school offerings. (Selectivity means the
number of students accepted compared to the number who
applied.) If you choose a highly selective school, you must
prepare yourself for rigorous academics. Highly selective
schools choose fewer applicants than less selective schools.
Keep in mind that except for highly selective schools, which
accept about half of the student applicants, a significant majority of U.S. colleges and universities accept 7 out of every
10 applicants (NCES, 2000), although those numbers change
when graduating high school seniors decide which school to
select. The yield, that is, the number of students who actually enroll, may be higher or lower. The popular perception
fueled by media, guidebooks, and the colleges themselves is
much more narrow or selective. It is true that many fresh-

men attend colleges that are their third or fourth choice, but from another perspective, there is a school for everyone who is willing to work hard.

Eventually you must narrow your options to between 5 and 10 colleges. To choose a list of 5 or 6 colleges that will be a good match for your interests and needs, you should know how colleges evaluate applicants so that you can compare your credentials with those of enrolled students.

- *Academic performance.* Every college first looks at a student's academic performance: the courses you took and the grades you earned in those courses. Many advanced courses are offered in sequence, so they will look first at 11th and 12th grade, and then look to see if there is an upward trend in the challenge level of the courses and the grades you earned. Every year of high school is important.

- *Standardized test scores.* Standardized tests (PSATs, SATs, ACTs, and SAT Subject Tests) are the only objective way a college can compare you to a student in some other part of the country. Most colleges want to know how successful you will be if you attend their college, and even if they don't request or use your scores, a low score on your transcript will get their attention and raise some questions. More information on the SATs and ACTs can be found in Appendix C.

- *Extracurricular activities.* After reviewing your academic performance and scores, admissions officers next look at your extracurricular activities and the way you spend your time when you are not in school. Colleges look for depth, commitment, initiative, and leadership, not for an exhaustive list.

- *Supporting material.* When highly selective colleges decide between two students who are on par academically, the creative presentation of extracurricular activities, the quality of recommendations, the essay or personal statement, the interview, and other written material can tip the balance in your favor.

Tips for Parents

As your family begins to talk about colleges, here are some things to watch for. Don't let your teen make these common college planning mistakes that students often make when choosing a list of colleges.

- Attempting to change oneself to fit to the college. A student may create five different "selves" to present to five different colleges. These students need assistance in presenting their true selves as accurately as possible.
- Abandoning common sense in investigating colleges. A college does not want to be evaluated solely on the basis of its students' SAT/ACT scores any more than you want to be evaluated solely on the basis of your SAT or ACT scores.
- Letting themselves be excessively influenced by college guidebooks and videos. These materials range in value, with some containing misleading information and others providing up-to-date, accurate information. Also, subjective books that evaluate colleges are often judgmental and may not state the criteria used for ranking schools.
- Spending too much time trying to gain a competitive edge in the process. Some students take the ACTs or SATs repeatedly or spend many hours thinking about a part of the process that is less important than grades or other standardized tests.
- Letting the results of the college admission process affect a student's self-esteem.

Parents, when your student is comfortable with a self-evaluation process and begins to view himself in terms of his values, interests, skills, and personal needs rather than in terms of his strengths and weaknesses, he is prepared to begin the exploration of college offerings. The better the self-knowledge the student has, the better the student will be able to match his or her goals, expectations, and requirements with those of a college. This matching process carries several cautionary notes.

Educators and counselors interviewed for this book indicated that gifted students become anxious about applying to college as early as seventh grade, although they may not know basic college planning facts, such as what courses will appear on a high school transcript. They need reassurance; for example, remind them that college decisions do not have to be made prior to 11th or 12th grade. However, reassurance unaccompanied by information and a coherent plan is rarely sufficient for gifted students.

Gifted students need to understand that college planning is part of a lengthy career planning process; it need not be a finite event that begins and ends mysteriously or arbitrarily. Learning about colleges is one part of a broad-based approach to planning for college, designing career goals, and, ultimately, leading a personally satisfying life.

During their latter years of high school, some gifted students seem to perfect the art of procrastination. Multipotential students may not be ready to select priorities; they may be academically successful in all courses while unable to focus. Students sensitive to the pressure of expectations may develop a case of advanced paralysis each time someone asks, "Where do you want to go to college?" Both groups swing from one unrealistic extreme to another. They decide on a college or career one day, and the next day they reject that choice and wonder how they will ever decide. These students may procrastinate until the 11th hour. Although this is common, parents become impatient as they realize the complexity of the application process and how little it resembles their own experiences. Parents may urge students to make an arbitrary decision based on cost or apply to colleges previously attended by family members, but if the match is to be a good one, the student should be the primary matchmaker.

The increasing number and variety of books on how to get accepted by the college of your choice add to everyone's anxiety. Students say these books are helpful because they learn how to market themselves. However, many books inadvertently reinforce the idea that college planning begins with November SATs or ACTs and ends with letters of acceptance from the student's chosen schools.

111

College and career planning may be particularly difficult for some gifted students. However, it can be a growth-promoting experience for all participants when the ultimate goal, student decisions based on realistic criteria that result in a satisfying life, is kept at the forefront of all decision-making activity.

Visiting Colleges

Applying to a college you haven't seen is like buying shoes by mail; it's simply impossible to know if you'll be comfortable.
—Dean of Admissions, small public university

Visiting colleges is Step 3 in your college search. You may have gathered a lot of information (Step 1) by reading the guides and asking questions. You may have started planning and choosing (Step 2) by comparing your scores to the scores of admitted students in some schools, or analyzing other types of information, such as the difference between selective or highly selective schools. Visiting colleges, however, is the only way to acquire firsthand information and test your conclusions, and it is the only justifiable way to make final college selection decisions. A visit offers an opportunity to look beneath the ivy and examine the bricks. If a campus visit isn't possible before you have to narrow your list of applications to five or six schools, you can always visit before you have to make a final choice.

Campus visits are most effective when conducted in two stages. Plan to collect different types of information during each stage. Timing depends on a number of things, including your schedule and your family's schedule. You should begin to visit campuses no later than your junior year in high school. If you want to consider applying for early decision, you must start earlier and/or combine the following steps.

Stage One Visits

You should plan to visit approximately 8 to 12 colleges that look interesting. Part of this tour is to compare colleges and universities and their differences. A college tour will be easier if the colleges you want to see are located in one state or adjoining states. A family-team approach works best for this type of "grand tour." If you have younger siblings, take them along, because they might notice things that you do not see and the trip will help them become familiar with college campuses. Be sure to go online for a campus map for each school you plan to visit.

Call each admissions office in advance and ask some of the following questions:

- Where is the nearest place to stay overnight?
- Are there any other colleges nearby?
- Will we be able to park on campus?
- What time are guided tours and group information sessions? How long do they last?
- Are students enrolled in the regular fall or spring semester currently taking classes on your campus?
- Are any campus activities planned on the day we plan to visit?
- Does the school offer on-campus interviews? If I want a personal interview with the dean of admissions or a representative, can you make suggestions about timing?

During the campus visit, you and your family should plan to accomplish the following:

- Take the guided tour.
- Visit several campus buildings.
- Eat in the dining halls.
- Read the student newspaper and bulletin boards.
- Ask questions of the admissions office, students, and faculty.
- Tour the surrounding area. Ask questions about the weather, shopping, and the community.
- Take good notes during each visit; record your impressions as soon as possible. Pick up an application and other information.

113

If the first visit includes a personal interview, write a prompt thank-you note to the interviewer. The personal note will reinforce the interviewer's memory of you and can be especially helpful if you are interviewed on a day when the admissions officer has seen many applicants.

If a trip is well-planned and you take good notes, you will gather a lot of informal information in a short time. A word of caution: If an initial visit is planned for summer, the students on campus may not be typical of the student body present during the regular term. The goal of the first visit, however, is to collect general information and answer the question, "Do I think I would be happy here?" You may require a second visit to secure specific information, present your student credentials to the college, and ask, "What are my chances for admission to this school?"

Following the first visits, sift through the information collected, talk with your parents and counselor, and narrow the list of possibilities. You should now be able to prepare a rank-ordered list of four to six colleges where you will probably be comfortable. If this is not possible, then additional campus visits or a different approach to analyzing the information gathered is necessary. It's better not to make a final decision on the basis of the first visit, especially if you did not stay in a dormitory.

Stage Two Visits

The second visit helps you reach final decisions. Here, timing may be more important than for the first visit. A stage two visit during late winter or early spring helps both you and the colleges. Between January (the date when most student applications must reach a college) and April (the month when colleges traditionally send out acceptance letters), colleges have the most information about their pool of applicants, available scholarship money, and other factors. They may be able to provide you with concrete information that will help you reach a final decision. Therefore, after completing the application process, you should try to revisit the campuses that interest you for at least 1 to 2 days each, preferably while classes are in session. Use the questions in this guide and the information you have gathered to develop a list of key questions to ask during this second visit.

Guidelines

Call well in advance to make an appointment to visit with college representatives, especially if you want an interview with an admissions officer, faculty member, and/ or the director of financial aid. It may be difficult to meet with some college representatives and admissions officers between August and December, because they tend to visit public and private high schools during the fall. You can visit on a day when most high schools are closed (e.g., a legal holiday). Make an appointment 3 or 4 months in advance. Some things you should do on your second visit include:

- Plan to spend enough time to experience "a day in the life of a student."
- Eat in the student dining halls again.
- Sit in on at least one class.
- Spend a night in a dorm room.
- Spend some time in the student center.
- Ask students why they decided to attend that particular school.
- Read bulletin boards and student newspapers.
- Plan to visit faculty members in academic or arts departments that interest you. Speak with athletic coaches and others who can provide information that will help you make your decision.
- Plan to present final credentials such as musical compositions, portfolios, and evidence of recent achievements.
- When in doubt, ask. No question is too dumb or unimportant in this process. Always get the name of the person you are talking to in case you have questions at a later time.
- If necessary, speak to the director of financial aid. Ask about merit- or talent-based scholarships.
- Recheck questions written prior to the visit; make sure they are all answered.

- Be sure to double-check the college's policy on the use of test scores such as AP Exams and SAT Subject Tests. Some colleges specify the subject tests they require for admission or placement; others allow applicants to choose which tests to take.

The campus visit will:
- provide firsthand information on colleges and what is expected of students;
- allow you to absorb something of the academic, social, and cultural atmosphere of the college;
- provide information about where college students eat, sleep, study, worship, attend classes, and relax;
- permit you to talk with college students, observe their lifestyles, see how they dress, and observe how they treat each other;
- provide firsthand information about the community in which a college is located; and
- give you an opportunity to size up the college in light of your personal goals.

The fact is, no matter how great a school looks on paper, it may not be right for you. If the field that interests you is a field where "connections" are crucial, or if you need to meet and work with people in your field before you graduate, a scholarship from a school that can't do that doesn't mean much.

Questions to Ask During a Campus Visit

The following list of suggested questions includes criteria you will find in any good college planning book. It also includes the general and specific questions gifted students should ask when investigating and analyzing colleges. Gifted students who are planning campus visits may wish to use the list to check off categories of personal importance. For example, a student who is primarily interested in the quality of the faculty at the colleges he or she applies to may use the list of questions in that category. Some students may find the list useful when they attempt to dispel myths that accompany college planning decisions: Questions about terms such as *intimate school size, rural pristine setting,* or *selective* may have some surprise answers.

It is important to understand that there are no perfect questions and no right or wrong answers. It is your responsibility to learn everything you can about a school you may attend for 4 or more years. No one would expect you to ask every one of the questions that follow, or to use their exact words. The questions are merely meant to guide your thinking as you read the college guides or use college selection software programs, visit campuses, and talk to college students, alumni, faculty, administrators, and others. Select the groups of questions that are important about college to you and your parents and concentrate your questions in those areas.

Questions About the Goals of a College

- What are the implicit and explicit missions and goals of the college or university? Does the school accommodate students who prefer to develop their intellectual abilities and judgment, as well as those who want to train for a specific profession? Does the college provide a climate that encourages students to think clearly and independently, to integrate the disciplines, and to become life-long learners on behalf of the common good?
- To what degree does the college or university make students aware that they are connected to a united intellectual and social community? How does the school encourage community service?
- To what degree does the college or university celebrate human diversity and allow for individual differences? What resources exist for gifted students who have disabilities, those from ethnic and multicultural groups, and other historically bypassed groups?

117

Questions About How a College Does Business

- How does the college or university ease the student's transition from secondary school, to higher education, to career paths?

- How are students recruited? How does the college expect promotional materials and recruitment strategies to shape student expectations? How do college representatives answer sharply focused questions about admission procedures (e.g., the use of standardized test scores and other student information)?
- How does the college or university show commitment to its enrolled students? Are students involved in governing the school? What resources does the school provide for academic advising, personal counseling, and career counseling? Does the school exhibit the same level of commitment toward preparing enrolled students for a personally satisfying life as it does toward recruiting new students and ensuring continued alumni financial support?

Questions About a College's Image or Reputation

- If the college or university is a prestigious school such as Harvard, Princeton, or Yale, how is prestige maintained and why do *you* want to attend? Is the college best known for academics? Specific academic areas? Athletics? Does the school have a reputation for producing scholars and statesmen?
- If the school is a relatively small school known for its personal attention to students, is it financially sound? Do alumni provide strong financial support for academic programs? Does the size of the student body indicate stability?
- Is the curriculum stable, or has it varied widely from year to year?

Questions About Demographics and Campus Geography

Location

- Is the school setting urban, rural, or suburban? Urban environments usually provide museums, terrific restaurants, and nightlife. When a town exists primarily because a college or university is there, you might have fewer choices when it comes to concerts and other cultural events.

- What are the specific advantages and disadvantages of each setting? Does *urban* mean that you can find a particular kind of food you like, but you will have to learn ways to protect yourself when you walk home from the library at night? Does *rural* mean that when you leave campus, everything that moves has four legs? Or, that the local town consists of a grocery store and a gas station?
- What methods of transportation exist if you want to go home on weekends or during brief school breaks? If you want to visit friends at another college? How often might you want to go home?
- What community resources exist near the school? Are there any museums nearby? Any specialty libraries?
- What is the *psychological* distance from home? If you attend a school where getting to transportation (train, plane) takes several hours, the psychological distance might be greater than the actual distance.
- How long will it take for a package to reach you?
- If you have been a part of the same group for a long time, do you need to go to school relatively far from home in order to try new activities and ideas?

Size
- Is the school small? Medium? Large? Huge? Gigantic? If it is a large school, can students register for courses over the Internet?
- How large are classes in each academic area? How does class size affect the quality and quantity of student participation? For example, are large lectures accompanied by study groups or some other means of reducing class size so that students can discuss class topics? If the school is relatively small, are prerequisite courses offered every semester?
- How is the campus designed? Is it compact? Spread out? Where are the dormitories in relation to classrooms? How long does it take to get to and from the library? Dining halls? Gymnasium? If the area gets a lot of snow, the daily hike to class or labs might take more time.
- What is the ratio of males to females?

119

- What is the percentage of culturally diverse students? What ethnic groups are represented?
- What is the percentage of undergraduates?
- What percentage of undergraduates commute?
- Does the school offer student seminars or other ways for students to work and learn together? Do faculty members lead the seminars?
- To what degree does campus size affect the facilities provided for student use? If a school boasts of superior technology and research facilities, who has access to them? Graduate students? Upperclassmen? Everyone who has ability, skill, and interest?

Costs

- What is the real meaning of *private*? *State-supported*? *Heavily endowed*?
- How are fees constructed? What are the added costs: student activity fees, lifestyle expenses, and books? Some textbooks cost more than $100 and the cost increases each year. Does the school bookstore sell used books?
- Are loans, scholarships, student aid, and work-study programs available? To whom? What are the requirements and limitations?
- Does the school provide work choices, or do the students have to find the jobs? Are there businesses outside the school (e.g., stores, restaurants) that offer part-time jobs to students?

Questions About Academic Life
Selectivity

- What is the college's rate of return for its freshman class? One of the best ways to measure a school's quality and the satisfaction of its students is to look at the percentage of students who return after the first year and the percentage of entering students who remain there until graduation. If you have selected a college major, look at the department's graduation rate. Typically, large state schools with an open-door admissions policy lose more students after their first year than smaller schools or those that are highly selective. This will impact class size and the use of facilities.

- How are student admissions folders read and evaluated? What relative weight is assigned to objective and subjective information? To numerical factors, such as GPA, class rank, and standardized tests? To subjective information, such as interviews, essays, presentation of special talents, and extracurricular activities?
- Are there quotas for in-state and out-of-state students? For specific geographic areas? For religious, economic, or ethnic groups? For students whose families are legacies and financial contributors?
- How are AP, ACT, and SAT Subject Test scores used? For credit? For exemption? For placement?

Course offerings
- What major fields of study are offered?
- How is each academic department ranked?
- What are the number and variety of distribution requirements (required courses)?
- What is the relative level of difficulty in specific academic departments?
- How and when do students select an academic major?
- Does each academic major broaden rather than restrict the student?
- How are students advised within each academic major?
- Can students select an academic major and retain flexibility to pursue career goals, as well as explore other areas of knowledge?
- How difficult is it to change majors?
- To what degree does each academic department prepare students for economic, social, and technological change?
- What are the maximum and minimum number of courses students may take each semester? How long is a semester?
- Does the school provide opportunities for students to enroll in courses offered by other colleges and universities? Is the school part of a consortium?

121

- Does the school offer a foreign study program? What are its requirements and/or limitations?
- Are undergraduate students encouraged to do independent research and self-directed study under the guidance of faculty mentors?
- Are students required to complete a thesis or senior seminar prior to graduation? If so, does the school state the purpose of the thesis or seminar? Is the purpose consistent with the school's stated mission and goals?
- Does the school provide opportunities for students to apply what they learn either in or out of the classroom?
- Are students required to own personal computers? Do students have to bring their own software? Who can use the school's computer system? Graduate students only? Underclassmen? Any student with ability, skill, and interest? Is the number of terminals sufficient to accommodate students during peak periods?
- Where are the computer terminals located in relation to other campus facilities? What time does the computer lab open and close?
- What percentage of funds does the school allocate to its library collection? To the library building?
- Are there a sufficient number of copies of required readings and library seats during peak periods?
- Is sufficient laboratory space available to accommodate the students enrolled in laboratory courses?

Academic atmosphere
- What is the level of competition at the school? Laid back? Cutthroat? What do enrolled students say about competition in classes? If the curriculum is highly rigorous, are you well-prepared?
- Does the school have an honors system or code of conduct? If so, how do students feel about it? Are standards enforced consistently?
- How does the school encourage creativity?

Faculty

- Who teaches undergraduates? Professors? Graduate assistants? Who teaches freshmen?
- What does the school expect of its faculty? How does the school encourage and reward faculty?
- What is the primary emphasis of the school? Scholarship? Research? Publications? How is good teaching encouraged? By student evaluations? Peer evaluations?
- How does the school encourage professional growth?
- What do students and faculty members say about the promotion and tenure system?
- What percentage of the faculty are part-time or adjunct instructors who do not have offices on campus?
- When are most faculty members available for student conferences and discussions? Only during office hours? At home? By telephone? Are teachers visible in dining halls and student centers?
- What is the relationship between faculty and students? Are most faculty members available outside of class?
- What opportunities exist for contact with faculty in your desired academic department?

Grading policies

- What grading system does the school use? A–F only? Pass/fail? Can the students go ungraded? Are there written evaluations?

Time structure (particularly important for students who prefer depth to scope of learning)

- Does the school operate on the semester system? Quarter system? Trimester system?
- Does the school offer a minisemester, such as an intense 1-month term in January or May that students can use to improve their grades or enrich their education?
- How many classroom hours are required each semester to graduate in 4 years?

123

Questions About Student Life

Orientation procedures

- How does the school acquaint freshmen with campus life, rules, and resources?
- Does the school hold a freshman convocation or have any procedure for celebrating the entrance of each new class?
- How do freshmen register for classes? Do they meet with an adviser prior to registration?
- How much assistance can they reasonably expect during the first year? If a student experiences severe academic difficulty, will an adviser call to offer assistance?

Social structure and campus life

- Consider what your college life will be like beyond the classroom. Aim for a balance between academics, activities, and social life. Before choosing a college, learn the answers to these questions:
  - What extracurricular activities, academic competitions, athletics, and special interest groups are available?
  - Does the community welcome students?
  - Is there an ethnic or religious group in which to take part?
  - How do fraternities and sororities influence campus life?
  - Is housing guaranteed?

- To what degree does the school encourage students to share their talents with others? Are faculty and students encouraged to volunteer for community service projects both within and outside of the school?
- To what degree do students participate in campus matters, particularly academic affairs?
- Does the school provide a climate in which all individuals are encouraged to work toward shared objectives?
- How does the school convey the prevailing rules system to students? Are the rules rigid? Loose?
- To what degree does the college tolerate or encourage student activism? Who controls the student newspaper?

- What is the policy on alcohol and substance use and abuse and what happens to students who break the rules? Is the campus dry? What about sororities and fraternities?
- What living arrangements does the college offer? Are coed and single-sex dormitories available to all? What is the policy regarding privacy versus open visitation?
- What percentage of the students commute, and where do they live? If the majority of students commute, this will impact campus life. In addition, commuting students may be older than typical college students.
- To what degree does the economic status of the student body influence campus life and/or activities? Are students asked to pay for every event?
- Is the school homogeneous or heterogeneous? If you attend a homogeneous school, you can expect that students will be similar to one another in some important ways. For example, everyone may dress alike because a particular style is popular. If you attend a heterogeneous school, you can expect everyone will do "their own thing." An example of a heterogeneous school is a very large state university. An example of a homogeneous school is a small liberal arts college. Do all students feel comfortable, regardless of lifestyle preference? Heterogeneous schools tend to foster leadership more so than homogeneous schools, so if you are a natural leader, you might be more comfortable at a school where leadership emerges quickly.
- How is the food on campus? Does the food taste good? Is the food good for you? Is there a variety of student dining halls?
- To what degree does the school encourage nonacademic campuswide activities that promote a sense of community?
- What organizations, clubs, and honor societies are available? For socializing? For career planning? For religious practice? Do faculty members attend these organizations on a regular basis?
- Does the school offer planned events on most weekends? If so, what kind of events? Would you attend?

- What provisions exist for student entertainment? On the campus? Off the campus? Is the school a party school? How do the students spend their leisure time?

Campus security
- Are personal belongings safe if left unattended in dormitory rooms and classrooms?
- What provisions are made to ensure student safety?
- Is it safe and acceptable to walk from the library to the dormitory alone? If not, what provisions are offered to protect personal safety?

Health
- What provisions does the school offer to assist students with physical and mental health?
- How is the student health center staffed? With nurses only? Is a physician on duty at all times?
- How far is the nearest well-equipped hospital?
- Does the student health service provide a comprehensive health education program and preventive medical advice? Does it provide help with stress? Assistance with personal health questions? Is personal counseling available? If so, what services are provided and what are the qualifications of the staff?

Study skills
- What facilities are available to students who want to improve their study skills?
- Does the school offer instruction in different study skills in each academic area?

Career guidance
- How does the school help students choose a career? Get a job? Select a graduate or professional school?
- What are the school's most recent experiences in placing alumni in graduate schools, professional schools, or jobs?
- Are internships and cooperative programs available in specific curricular areas?

Questions for Gifted Students With Disabilities
- How does the school encourage special groups of students to enroll?
- What specific provisions exist for meeting the special academic, physical, and social needs of these students?
- What is the school's retention rate for students with disabilities?

Visiting colleges is just one step in the college planning process that should take place during your junior and senior years of high school. Because the junior year is an essential time to begin planning for college, this book provides a detailed checklist of the steps you need to take care of during your junior year in Appendix D. This checklist will ensure smooth planning, and help you organize your time, so you can visit the colleges of your choosing.

Student-Athletes: Choosing and Visiting Prospective Colleges

Student-athletes, or at least those who wish to play varsity sports at the collegiate level, have additional considerations to plan for when choosing a college. Although a college may recruit you, instead of you seeking out the college, you still need to ensure that you make the right fit for you academically, emotionally, and socially. You should make sure that you follow the same principles set forth for other students in this book, asking relevant questions, visiting colleges and experiencing all you can on campus, and taking time to make a good, sound decision. There are, however, some very specific things college-bound student-athletes must do in the college planning process.

When you first begin to wonder if you might be eligible for collegiate-level sports, visit the National Collegiate Athletic Association's (NCAA) Web site (http://www.ncaa.org). The NCAA governs all varsity-level intercollegiate sports

127

at more than 1,200 colleges nationwide, and its Web site provides student-athletes with plenty of good information about the rules and procedures behind the athlete recruiting process. It's also a good idea to download a copy of the organization's free *Guide for the College-Bound Student-Athlete* (NCAA, 2005) from its Web site.

If you wish to participate in varsity sports during your first year of college, you *must* first register with the NCAA Initial-Eligibility Clearinghouse, an organization that will determine your eligibility for participation in NCAA sports. This organization looks at each student's high school academic records, ACT or SAT scores, and whether the student qualifies as an amateur athlete. To participate in college-level sports, students must be determined to be an amateur by the NCAA Clearinghouse; in other words, the organization will review your records for issues such as a contract with a professional sports team, receiving a salary for participating in athletics, preferential treatment based on your athletics reputation, and benefits from prospective professional sports agents (NCAA, 2005).

Students who are determined to be eligible for varsity sports by the Clearinghouse can then move on to the next steps: visiting and/or being recruited by college sports programs. It's important for student-athletes to review the recruiting regulations for college sports as laid out in the *Guide for the College-Bound Student-Athlete* (NCAA, 2005). A number of rules and regulations apply to this process, and it's important to make sure you follow each one carefully. Many schools encourage students to send videotapes of their high school playing time to the prospective sport's recruiting office. Coaches and assistants review these tapes often, and, although a coach will not make a decision to recruit you based solely on your taped performance, the videotape may alert him or her to your abilities, making you a potential recruit he or she had not seen or considered beforehand.

Often, college coaches pay close attention to various high schools' performance each season. Coaches know the area they recruit from well, visiting schools in their region often, reading newspapers and Internet recounts of the local sports, and reviewing tapes of student-athletes who play in their regions. It's likely that if you are a standout athlete at a top-performing school, coaches from several universities are already aware of your abilities. However, no matter your performance record, reputation, or abilities, the recruiting process remains the same; NCAA rules do not allow for any special or preferential treatment for college athletes at any time. The recruiting process includes several important events, including the initial contact, the evaluation period, and the official visit.

Contact is a term used by NCAA to describe any time when a coach has any face-to-face contact with you or your parents off of the college's campus. During the *contact period*, a college coach may have in-person contact with you and/or your parents on or off of the college's campus; this means the coach may watch you play or visit you at your high school, he or she may write or telephone you, and you and your parents may visit a college campus during this time. The *evaluation* takes place when a college evaluates your athletic and academic ability, either by visiting your high school or watching you practice or compete. However, during the *evaluation period*, the coach may watch you play, but he or she cannot have any in-person contact with you or your parents off of the college campus. Another important part of the recruiting process is the *official visit*, which occurs any time you and your parents visit the college, and the college pays for your expenses, such as transportation and meals (NCAA, 2005). These are only a few of the specific terms and stages related to the recruiting process; for more information, refer to the NCAA's *Guide for the College-Bound Student-Athlete.*

While gathering information about and considering various colleges, there are certain, specific questions you should ask the coaches to help you make a sound decision about your future. Some questions you should consider asking include (NCAA, 2005):

- What position(s) will I play on your team?
- What expectations do you have for training and conditioning?
- How would you best describe the staff's coaching style?

129

- How many credit hours should I take in and out of season?
- Are there restrictions in scheduling classes around practice?
- What is a typical day like for a student-athlete?
- Must student-athletes live on campus?
- What kind of athletic scholarships are available? What do they cover? What do they not cover?
- Under what circumstances would my scholarship be reduced or canceled?
- What scholarship money is available after my eligibility is over to help me complete my degree? (NCAA student-athletes are only eligible for 4 years of play. Some degrees, such as many engineering programs, take longer than 4 years to complete. If you are thinking about a major that might take you longer than 4 years to complete, this is a good question to ask.)

Again, if you're considering playing sports in college, the best thing to do is to check out the NCAA's Web site for specific information, rules, and regulations. If you aren't recruited for a varsity team, but don't want to give up sports, don't be discouraged. Many schools operate university-governed club sports teams that compete against other nearby schools (at many schools, traditional varsity sports like volleyball and softball are also offered as club sports, along with others like rugby, lacrosse, and cycling), and most large universities have very competitive intramural sports programs (where clubs, student-organized teams, and dorms compete against one another) for sports like flag football, volleyball, 3-on-3 basketball, slow pitch softball, and soccer. Be sure and ask about these various athletic opportunities available on campus during your campus visit.

5

The Application Process: What Do I Have That They Want?

Chapter 5 completes the college matching process by answering the questions "What do I have that they want?" and "How can I show them in the application process?" In addition, this chapter covers the final four steps of the college planning process: applying, interviewing and writing an essay, applying for financial aid, and making acceptance decisions. The application process is discussed from two points of view: that of the multipotential gifted student, who may be able to make rational choices, but whose options are infinite; and that of the admissions officer, who may have to select the freshman class from a wide range of highly qualified applicants.

The five elements of a successful application process are a student's grades, GPA, and class ranking; standardized test scores; activities and experiences; the application essay; and recommendations. Each element is important for students who are drawn to the most highly selective schools. Keep in mind the following:

- Some gifted students are drawn to the most selective colleges and universities. Any student planning to apply to a highly selective school must understand two things: There is no such thing as *the perfect school,* and the way the student addresses the application process may be the critical factor determining acceptance or rejection.

- If a student decides to attend college before graduating from high school, parents should assess the student's ability to live away from the family, establish social relationships in college, and set long-term goals. The pros and cons of attending an online university should be weighed, along with other possibilities such as early entrance programs.
- When gifted students decide to apply to selective colleges, they may have to be led through the application process. They may not understand the importance of documenting activities. They may need an educational consultant's assistance or one of the many summer camp experiences that offer college planning activities.
- Colleges are usually looking for a well-rounded student body. What does that mean? Students frequently join every activity available in an effort to appear well-rounded, but colleges would rather see fewer activities and concentrated commitment toward one or two. When the college decides on the incoming freshman class, there will be students with a variety of skills. There will be musicians; sports enthusiasts; academic super achievers; students from rural areas, the city, and suburbs; and students from many income levels, countries, and cultures; in other words, a well-rounded, diverse student body.

College Admission Prep Camps and Independent College Planning Consultants

Travel to Tufts University or UCLA during the summer and you will see a college admission prep camp in action. College admission has become so competitive that some parents and students are no longer willing to approach it without professional help. Talking to an admissions counselor, reading college publications, or practicing the SAT or

ACT at home is not enough to reduce the angst for some families, especially those with students applying to highly selective colleges.

Students need more refined tools if they are to apply to a highly selective school. An increasingly popular solution is college prep camps (Hansen, n.d.). They are run by private companies and college counseling organizations, and are scattered throughout the nation. Students can enroll in a prep camp and get individual instruction on their college essay, take an SAT or ACT prep course, receive one-on-one college counseling, and get help with study skills and time management. However, this approach does not come cheap. The college prep camps run by Education Unlimited (see http://educationunlimited.com) at campuses throughout the nation cost upwards of $2,250 for 10 days. Most of the private companies host small groups of students who spend 12 hours a day, every day, taking classes or receiving individual help on college planning. Most students have no idea how to approach the admissions process, and with an average student-counselor ratio of 1 to 500 in public schools, they are unlikely to get what they need from overworked guidance counselors. When exploring these camps, make sure you are getting the return you are looking for.

Another approach to the college planning process is engaging the services of a private counselor to provide one-on-one counseling. *Independent counselors* and *educational consultants* are two different terms used to describe a counselor/adviser outside of the school setting who assists students and parents with the college admission process for a fee. Usually, they prefer to begin a program no later than a student's sophomore year, and work with the student until his or her applications have been sent, although most people begin later. You should always ask for qualifications, including personal references. And, you should interview more than one consultant, because you are looking for a knowledgeable person who will "click" with your son or daughter. This person is going to help your teen find a suitable match between personal goals and college offerings. The relationship is therefore important.

133

Independent counselors spend time visiting colleges and universities, and frequently have relationships with admissions staff members. Experienced counselors often know the type of student a particular college is looking for. And, they are usually on mailing lists and have access to information others don't have. For example, one U.S. college takes great pride in its bagpipe band. One year, most of the band members graduated, and the university sent out a notice that they would award a full tuition, room, and board scholarship to students who were qualified academically and had some expertise playing a bagpipe. Such unusual, but rewarding information given to private consultants and college counselors can pay off, and may make it well worth the costs of hiring outside advisers.

Two national associations grant membership specifically to independent college counselors based on set criteria. If you have questions about those criteria, or if you are looking for a consultant, contact the following nonprofit membership organizations:

- National Association for College Admission Counseling
  1631 Prince Street
  Alexandria, VA 22314-2818
  (800) 822-6285
  http://www.nacacnet.org
- Independent Educational Consultants Association
  3251 Old Lee Highway Ste. 510
  Fairfax, VA 22030-1504
  (800) 808-IECA
  http://www.educationalconsulting.org

Before you invest in a private counselor or camp, you may want to become familiar with the process, as well as local resources. Only then can you decide whether your teen needs outside help.

A Look at the Application

We begin with a look at the application and the process by which candidates are evaluated. Two kinds of information are required on the typical college application form: objective and subjective. Objective information includes biographical data, information on academic performance, standardized test scores such as SATs or ACTs, AP Exam grades, and additional numerical information. Subjective information includes extracurricular activities, recommendations, the essay and/or personal statement, and a personal interview. Depth and scope of extracurricular activity are preferred to a "laundry list" of activities. Colleges are particularly interested in a student's initiative, leadership ability, and indication of community service.

When the academic credentials of two applicants are roughly equal, subjective information and the student's method of presentation become deciding factors. (Sometimes a student's geographic location, the school his or her parents attended, or particular talents can tip the balance in favor of or against acceptance.) The more applicants a college has for each place in its entering class, the more selective that college can and will be. At highly selective colleges, virtually all of the application folders contain outstanding credentials.

At this point, it's a good idea to begin organizing your application materials. Getting organized before you begin the procedure of applying to schools can ease some of the stress and tension you may feel later on. Knowing you have everything in order and under control can be very helpful when multiple application deadlines spring up at once. The application organizer in Figure 5 can help. You can make your own spreadsheet using Microsoft Excel™ or any spreadsheet program.

You will also want to create a folder for use in the application process, containing the following items:

135

College Applications	School Name	School Name	School Name
Application deadline			
Essay completed			
Application form completed			
Application mailed			
Notification date			
Financial Aid Applications			
Financial aid application deadline			
FAFSA mailed			
Completed PROFILE registration process			
PROFILE form mailed			
College's financial aid application mailed			
Recommendation Letters			
1. Gave recommendation form to: _____			
Writer mailed form or returned it to me			
Sent thank-you note			
2. Gave recommendation form to: _____			
Writer mailed form or returned it to me			
Sent thank-you note			

Figure 5. Application organizer

College Applications	School Name	School Name	School Name
3. Gave recommendation form to: _____			
Writer mailed form or returned it to me			
Sent thank-you note			
High School Transcripts			
Gave transcript to counselor			
Form mailed			
Gave midyear school report form to counselor			
Form mailed			
Test Scores			
Requested that score reports be sent to colleges			
SAT			
SAT Subject Tests			
ACT			
AP Exams			
IB			
Other			
Other			
Other			
Figure 5, continued			

137

- Recommendations from adult leaders of special programs in which you participated during 9th, 10th, and 11th grades. These should be obtained upon completion of the activity and placed in your file for possible use at a later time, but only if the adult knew you extremely well.
- Transcripts from out-of-school courses; course descriptions should be included also.
- Your application organizer, placed in a spot where it's easy to access (such as stapled to the front inside cover) and where you can see how you are progressing in the process.

Colleges look favorably upon transcripts showing increasing academic rigor during 4 years of high school. A quirk in the transcript (e.g., an atypical course or low grade in a challenging academic course) should be accompanied by an explanation, particularly if the event occurs during 11th or 12th grade. An example of a situation requiring explanation is a period of illness during which a student falls far behind in his or her work and receives a poor or failing grade. Explanations are also useful if a student experiences family problems, overcomes difficulties, or maintains his grades in spite of difficulties. You should address these situations in an essay or personal statement. If your transcript looks like a roller coaster or if you have a low grade in an academically challenging course, you need to explain.

Jorge missed more than half of the first semester of 12th grade because of illness. His teachers cooperated with him and he was able to keep up with the work, except for that in calculus. The calculus teacher was unwilling to prepare work to send home. When he returned to school, he received F's in calculus, but decided to stay in the class despite the unlikely possibility of raising his grade. His reason, he explained to his family, was that he was eventually going to need calculus, and he could learn more in that class than he could learn in a study hall, which was his only other choice. When he applied to colleges, he chose colleges that provided an opportunity to make a personal statement and he explained his situation. He was offered admission to four selective schools. The schools that rejected his application were those that conducted their initial screening by computer. His calculus grade knocked him out of competition for those schools, one of which was his "safety school."

The parts of the application should fit together to provide a common theme. Recommendations should support and be consistent with both the academic record and what the student says about him- or herself. Again, any quirk should be explained. For example, high SAT/ACT scores combined with a relatively low GPA or a high GPA and low SAT/ACT scores provide an inconsistent picture of an applicant; they may suggest a problem (e.g., high ability, but low motivation) to an admissions officer and need to be addressed in the application package or interview.

Documentation of activities may be critical to the admissions process. To document activities, students may, for example, enter a contest, submit work for publication, keep a scientific journal, or keep a notebook of artistic works. Active participation in a highly competitive individual or team sport should always be documented. But, know when to play it safe. When considering the use of gimmicks or attention-grabbers, be careful to distinguish between those that cause you to stick out and those that help you to stand out. Entering national competitions and contests is one way to help you stand out, while documenting your interests. A list of national competitions is included in Appendix E.

The following examples illustrate ways of documenting interests and proficiency.

139

Julie was a capable, academically successful student who aspired to attend a highly competitive college. At an early age, she became interested in race walking. She spent her leisure time perfecting this skill, but it never occurred to her to document her interest. Her counselor discovered Julie's interest and suggested that she enter a race walking competition. Much to Julie's surprise, she placed 25th in a regional competition. The contest added another dimension to her leisure interest and gave her an edge in the college application process.

Jon was a mathematically gifted student, but his grades were average because he spent most of his time creating and constructing puzzles of every variety imaginable. Jon explained his interest in a personal statement attached to his application and submitted a puzzle with the application. His puzzle consisted of some wood strips and a question. He asked whether or not anyone could construct a kinetic geometric model showing the "interpenetration and duality of the cube and the octahedron." He did not include the solution. The admissions officer contacted Jon to ask him how to solve the puzzle.

The Common Application

Counselors and parents may find that gifted students suddenly decide to apply to a particular college and have not sent for the application. In such a case, the Common Application may meet the needs of the student. The Common Application is a standardized application that is accepted by approximately 277 selective colleges and universities for admission to their undergraduate programs. Students complete one Common Application form, photocopy it, and send the form to any of the participating colleges. The procedure simplifies the college application process and eliminates duplication of effort. To further simplify the process, you can use the Common Application Web site (http://www.commonapp.org) to complete your forms and submit them electronically or in hardcopy. Or, download PDF forms to complete onscreen or manually, then print and mail the hardcopy to the school to which you're applying. The Common Application will save you time, but it may not always be the best choice. A student's individuality will come through most clearly when he or she chooses the avenues of communication with care. So, before you use the Common Application, compare it with each school's application form. Are they different? Which of the two would show off your talents to the fullest? Figure 6 is a sample copy of a page of the Common Application.

Electronic applications

Electronic applications have become a fairly popular method of applying to college. The college planning process has been thoroughly infused with technology. Schools distribute most of their information via Web site, including college costs, the college profile (e.g., SAT/ACT scores of current students), the course catalog, and detailed admission information. Schools receive more than half their applications electronically. There are usually two ways to do this: (1) download and print the application, complete it by hand, and mail it by postal service; (2) complete the application online and submit it electronically through the college's Web site. In addition, there are application services that will hold the information you send for use in several applications. Several of these services are listed in Appendix B of this book.

If you complete the application online, be sure you print a copy of everything you send. Then, follow up with a phone call or e-mail to make sure your application arrived and is intact. Using an electronic application process is great for some people, but you have to be careful to send the application well ahead of the deadline. Although technology has come a long way, there are no guarantees. One year, a university's server crashed as a result of the onslaught of applications sent electronically just before the deadline. On another occasion, an Internet service provider read acceptance letters from a highly selective school as spam, and deleted them. So, if you submit your application electronically, be sure to follow up.

141

COMMON APPLICATION™
2005–2006

APPLICATION FOR UNDERGRADUATE ADMISSION

The member colleges and universities listed above fully support the use of this form. No distinction will be made between it and the college's own form. Please type or print in black ink.
Be sure to follow the instructions on the cover page of the Common Application booklet to complete, copy, and file your application with any one or several of the member colleges and universities.

OPTIONAL DECLARATION OF EARLY DECISION/EARLY ACTION

Complete this section **ONLY** for the individual college to which you are applying ED or EA. It is your responsibility to follow that college's instructions regarding early admission, including obtaining and submitting any ED/EA form provided by that college. Do **NOT** complete this ED/EA section on copies of your application submitted to colleges for Regular Decision or Rolling Admission.

College Name _____ Deadline _____

☐ Early Decision ☐ Early Action ☐ EASC

PERSONAL DATA

Legal Name _____
Enter name exactly as it appears on passports or other official documents.   *Last/Family*   *First*   *Middle (complete)*   *Jr., etc.*   *Gender*

Nickname (choose only one) _____   Former last name(s) if any _____

Are you applying as a ☐ freshman or ☐ transfer student?   For the term beginning _____

Birthdate _____ *mm/dd/yyyy*   E-mail Address _____

Permanent Home Address _____ *Number and Street*

City or Town   *State/Province*   *Country*   *Zip Code or Postal Code*

Permanent Home Phone (_____) _____ *Area Code*   *Number*

If different from above, please give your mailing address for all admission correspondence.

Mailing Address (from _____ *(mm/yyyy)* to _____ *(mm/yyyy)*) _____ *Number and Street*

City or Town   *State/Province*   *Country*   *Zip Code or Postal Code*

Phone at mailing address (_____) _____ *Area Code Number*   Cell phone (_____) _____ *Area Code Number*

Citizenship ☐ US citizen   ☐ Dual US citizen; please specify other country of citizenship _____

☐ US Permanent Resident visa; citizen of _____   Alien Registration Number _____

☐ Other Citizenship _____ *Country(ies)* _____ *Visa type*

If you are not a US citizen and live in the United States, how long have you been in the country? _____

Possible area(s) of academic concentration/major(s) _____ or undecided ☐

Special college or division if applicable _____

Possible career or professional plans _____ or undecided ☐
Will you be a candidate for financial aid? ☐ Yes ☐ No   If yes, the appropriate form(s) was/will be filed on _____

The following items are *optional*. No information you provide will be used in a discriminatory manner.

Place of birth _____ *City State/Province Country*   Social Security Number (if any) _____

First language, if other than English _____   Language spoken at home _____

If you wish to be identified with a particular ethnic group, please check all that apply
☐ African American, Black   ☐ Mexican American, Chicano
☐ Native American, Alaska Native (tribal affiliation _____ enrolled _____)   ☐ Native Hawaiian, Pacific Islander
☐ Asian American (countries of family's origin _____)   ☐ Puerto Rican
☐ Asian, including Indian Subcontinent (countries _____)   ☐ White or Caucasian
☐ Hispanic, Latino (countries _____)   ☐ Other (specify _____)

2005–2006   AP-1

Figure 6. Common application sample page

Note. Used with permission from The Common Application, Inc.

How Candidates Are Evaluated

The following scene typifies an admissions office at a highly selective college or university.

The admissions counselor is sitting at his desk, which is piled high with application folders. He has read 40 applications today. It is now 10 p.m., and he would like to go home. Instead, he takes the next folder off the pile and reviews it as always, with no knowledge of the student—what the student is like, what the student has accomplished, what the student hopes to achieve, and what the student can contribute to the university or college. The admissions officer may spend no more than 5 or 10 minutes looking at the application during this first reading. The admissions officer will first look at the name of the student's school district to see whether he is familiar with the quality of the education provided there. He will then look at the student's high school profile to see if the high school has a challenging academic program, and finally will check the student's academic performance—courses taken and grades earned. He follows this pattern, because when a college accepts a student it gambles on the student's chances of succeeding at the school. A student who performs consistently well all through high school is a much lower risk than one whose performance has been erratic. Even though a student's record may identify him or her as gifted (or enrolled in a special program), colleges will evaluate the student's credentials in the same manner as those of all other students.

143

In some instances, computers perform initial reviews. Applicant data is entered into a computer formula and the computer recommends whether admission should be accepted or denied. The admission committee looks at the application and the computer-generated data before making a final decision. This process is a distinct disadvantage to a gifted student whose academic credentials—GPA, class rank, or standardized test scores—are not reflective of the student's ability and potential. It may also be a problem for students who are homeschooled.

Keep in mind that large state schools may have open admission, meaning they must admit any state resident who applies before a specific date. The more state residents who apply, the less chance there is that an out-of-state resident will be accepted. Such universities may be required to limit the number of students they accept from outside the state.

What Do Admissions Officers Look For?

Academic Performance

A student's academic performance consists of several factors: grade point average, class rank, and academic rigor. When looking at your grade point average and class rank a school will ask: How good are the student's grades, and where does the student stand compared to his or her classmates? When checking for academic rigor, an admissions officer will seek evidence of superior ability in the form of honors, an IB Program, or AP courses. Some colleges ignore honors or GT classes because they are of unknown quality. Students should be alert to the difference between state academic requirements for high school graduation and requirements for admission to a selective college. The most selective colleges are interested in evidence of high motivation and achievement—that is, high grades in very demanding courses. Taking AP courses, if available in the student's high school, demonstrates that the student is capable of performing at a high level of academic proficiency. AP grades of 3, 4, or 5 may be accepted for exemption from a university's required freshman courses and/or for college credit. Students, you should check a college's AP policy. You should not just assume that you will receive transcript credit or place out of freshman-level classes for your AP test scores. Academic rigor consists of the following elements:

- *Depth* in areas such as foreign languages and mathematics. Studying one language for 6 years is better than studying two languages for 3 years apiece.
- *Quality.* Did the student take four or five major subjects each year (English, mathematics, science, history, language) or a variety of nonacademic or elective courses (e.g., business law, fashion merchandising, culinary arts, study hall)? Course descriptions should reflect the rigor of each course. If a high school does not include course descriptions and a profile of school credentials with college applications, and course titles do not accurately reflect quality, the student or counselor should attach an explanation to the transcript. School credentials include factors like the number of students who take AP courses and the number of students who are eligible for free lunch because of their family's low income.
- *Balance.* Did the student take a broad curriculum (mathematics and science, history, and English courses) or concentrate too heavily in one area?
- *Trends.* Are the student's grades gradually improving or growing weaker each year? Recent performance is the most important indicator of the student's current level of ability and motivation.

One dean of admissions, when asked whether he would prefer to see a C in calculus or an A in a less rigorous course, replied "An A in calculus. If, however, the student takes rigorous courses in other disciplines, a C in calculus is better than a higher grade in a relatively easy mathematics course." Although the dean sidestepped the question, his response indicated that students should take the most rigorous courses offered by their high school. If the student's high school offered calculus, taking a less rigorous mathematics course would not be a good choice, even if it meant that the student would earn a higher grade. Grades aren't everything and rising to a challenge would be viewed as a positive step.

145

Standardized Test Scores

Standardized test scores (PSAT, SAT, ACT, etc.) supplement high school transcripts and permit an admissions officer to compare all applicants against a similar standard. These tests share a common characteristic: They are timed and yield a standardized score. The College Board may use several versions of the test on a given day, but all versions will be comparable. The verbal and mathematics portions are multiple-choice tests. When the PSATs and SATs were revised, more emphasis was placed on critical thinking skills in both the verbal and mathematical sections (College Board, n.d.b). The SAT now includes a 30-minute essay portion requiring students to write an essay that requires them to take a position on an issue and use reasoning and examples to support their position (College Board, n.d.a). At the same time, the ACT added a 30-minute writing test that measures writing skills emphasized in high school English classes and in entry-level college composition courses.

Selective schools may emphasize SAT Subject Test scores. Students may take one, two, or three tests each testing session. The only exception is for listening tests—students may take one listening test and two other subject tests. If you are taking a course in which you are doing quite well, consider taking a subject test if one is offered. Do not wait until your senior year to do so: You may forget what you have learned. In addition, you may want to take more than three subject tests, and, if you wait until senior year, this will be impossible. The SAT and SAT Subject Tests must be taken on separate testing dates.

Students who are considering taking the SAT Subject Tests should know that not all colleges require these exams. There is a list of schools and their subject test requirements online (http://www.ivywest.com/satiireq.htm), but you should check with each college that interests you. Schools will vary on how many subject tests applicants are required to take. In order to be sure you are meeting all requirements, check each individual school's testing requirements for details and plan ahead. A student who plans to take the SAT and three subject tests could take the SAT in May of his or her junior year, two subject tests in June, the SAT for a second time in October of his or her senior year and the remaining subject tests in November. That will leave the December test date to repeat any test where a higher score is desired.

Many Web sites offer students the opportunity to download, print, and take a free, full-length practice test. Some offer a review and skills report, and explanations to all test answers so students can see how and why they earned a particular score. In addition, Kaplan, the test preparation company, has a teenager-friendly answer to practicing for the SATs—test prep software that runs on handheld computers, cell phones and smart phones.

Some colleges prefer to see scores from the ACT. Like the SAT, the ACT assesses high school students' general educational development and their ability to complete college-level work. Unlike the SAT, the ACT includes multiple-choice tests that cover four skill areas: English, mathematics, reading, and science (ACT, n.d.a). The recently added 30-minute writing test is optional and measures skill in planning and writing a short essay. Each section of the test is scored from 1 to 36; then, those four section scores are averaged for a composite score. The maximum composite score a student can achieve on the ACT is 36, a score earned by approximately 1 in 6,000 high school graduates. Students who take the optional writing test receive all of the same scores that students who do not take the writing test receive. In addition, students who take the writing test receive a scaled score, ranging from 1–36, that reflects their performance on the writing test and the English Test combined, and constructive feedback on their writing in the form of reader comments (ACT, n.d.b)

Colleges vary in their use of standardized test scores. Some schools, believing that SAT and ACT scores predict college grades, use scores as one criterion for admission decisions. If you are not a good test taker, make sure that you prepare well and retake tests if needed, so your scores are not so low that you can be eliminated from consideration. Other schools place primary emphasis on high school academic achievement and AP and subject test scores, and

147

then look at subjective information such as the student essay. Students should ask college representatives how the various scores and tests are used in the college's admissions process.

Extracurricular Activities

Seth was interested in engineering. He knew that the field was changing, so during 10th grade he researched different types of engineering. He was fascinated with forensic engineering professionals who evaluate crime scene evidence to narrow the search for a criminal. He knew he wanted to be of service to humanity and thought about the possibility of becoming a pharmaceutical engineer, one who perhaps discovers a vaccine for a disease. He also liked designing things and was interested in robotics and aerodynamics. During 11th grade, he volunteered in a laboratory where vaccines were developed and realized that he felt good about himself and the problems that the scientists let him work on. Seth worked in the laboratory for the next 2 years. He applied to highly selective colleges and was accepted by most, because he had good grades in rigorous science and math courses. But, that wasn't all. The admissions officers saw that Seth had a track record in his chosen field and he had conducted some independent research, qualities that gave Seth an edge in a highly competitive admissions process.

Imagine the following scene: After the application deadline, an admissions committee reviews all applications by looking at each one for about 10 minutes. They know that they can accept about one student in six, so the first thing they do is divide the applications into three stacks. Some applications are immediately placed in a rejection pile because the students' academic credentials do not indicate future success at the school in question. But then, faced with a pile of acceptable applicants, the admissions officer picks a folder and says, "What makes you so special? Why should I accept you?" He is going to try to determine how the applicant spends his or her time outside the classroom and what these activities say about the applicant.

Most selective colleges ask students to list, describe, and sometimes comment on the significance of their extracurricular activities. They are interested in depth of commitment, personal initiative, originality, leadership ability, and evidence of a social conscience. An applicant does not need an exhaustive list to have an impact. In fact, membership in several student organizations is less impressive than a major contribution to one organization or activity. This means that you do not have to hold an office in every club or be captain of every team. Admissions officers want to see whether or not you can pursue an activity and acquire expertise in it. They also look for leadership and evidence that you have shared your talents and expertise with others. Extracurricular activities demonstrate skills and abilities that cannot be seen on a student's transcript. This information rounds out an application.

Some students pursue solitary interests; they might be computer hackers, basement scientists, or midnight poets. Your particular interest will be easier to discuss if it is documented in some way. You can avoid a last-minute flurry of activity by keeping a journal of your progress, keeping a notebook of your poems, entering a contest, or finding some method to convey to colleges that your interest in an activity did not begin and end when you realized you needed to list activities on your application. Well-rounded activities indicate a student's interest in a variety of endeavors, but intense concentration in one or two areas, if properly documented, is more likely to be impressive, especially if the activity is related to a student's career goals.

149

For example, when asked on the college application to "describe the importance of a sport or sports to you and discuss what you feel you've gained from participation in sports," a student admitted to a highly selective college, replied, in part, with the following statement:

It was very important for me to get involved in sports when I started high school. I was short for my age and somewhat shy. To be part of a team and to get to know and trust your teammates at a time when you need all the friends you can get was invaluable. As a freshman, making the freshman basketball team really helped me fit in and feel comfortable in high school. I discovered you don't have to be the team superstar to make being there worthwhile. At 14, I was only 5'2" and saw very little court time, but it was probably more rewarding for me to be there than my taller teammates and to have accomplished my preseason goal of making the team. I was certainly the shortest one trying out for the team that year, and I was very nervous, yet I never gave up and I never stopped hustling. Making the team that year gave me the confidence to do other things that made me nervous.

The rest of the student's statement briefly described the frustrations, trials, and tribulations encountered through 4 years of high school athletics and clearly indicated what he learned from his years of participation in different sports. Additional personal statements in his application indicated that the student was a successful problem solver.

Technology has introduced a new dimension to documenting extracurricular activities. Applicants can produce multimedia DVDs illustrating their skills and abilities. However, any media presentation of skills is effective only if it demonstrates an aspect of the student's ability that cannot be demonstrated in any other way and relates to the student's ability to perform in college. Using multimedia does not necessarily demonstrate the capacity to be original and creative; it is a means to an end rather than an end in itself. The following examples illustrate this point.

Josh was an expert windsurfer. The admissions office received a professional-quality DVD showing Josh successfully navigating his way through relatively difficult surf. Although it was interesting, the presentation had little impact on the deliberations of the admissions committee. If, however, Josh added a narrative describing the way windsurfing relates to his interest in physics, he would have provided necessary meaning to his interest and credentials.

Dora's primary strength was her sense of humor and natural artistic ability. She was often bored in class and drew satirical cartoons while teachers lectured. When Dora applied to selective colleges, she capitalized on her abilities by producing an animated cartoon. Her theme, school politics, cast some of her teachers in a rather poor light, but it reflected her ability to use technology effectively and her ability to cope with some negative educational experiences through her sense of humor. Counselor recommendations provided consistency by discussing Dora's sense of humor and ability to deal with diverse situations.

Dora was interested in animation and marketing and applied to a college that was known for nurturing students interested in technology and business. Because Dora chose an appropriate college, the admissions officer understood her experiences and her sense of humor as portrayed in the presentation. He predicted that she would blossom in his university environment. The admissions committee was impressed with Dora's honesty and creativity. The submission, then, made a difference.

Submitting material that provides evidence of talent can be tricky. Admissions officers are flooded with DVDs, portfolios, and home-baked bread. Talent definitely counts, especially in the arts. However, students should ask whether or not the college will accept supplementary material and how they can best present extracurricular activities and special talents. Any method that demonstrates the student's ability to perform in college and adds substance and consistency to the application is desirable.

When the student, guidance counselor, and parents agree to send supporting material, care must be taken in the presentation of that material:

- Send evidence, not testimony.
- Submit the best work in a concise form. Keep it short and to the point.
- Be sure that the supplementary material adds something to the application that cannot be illustrated in any other way, and that it demonstrates, in some way, the student's ability to succeed at the school. This does not mean that a student should submit an application with only a simple description of activities; it simply means that evaluation and informed judgment should guide the presentation of material.
- When in doubt, spell it out. Don't use acronyms or abbreviations. The person reading your application may not understand the terms.

When highly selective colleges decide between two very qualified students who are on par academically, the creative presentation of extracurricular activities, the quality of recommendations, the essay or personal statement, the interview, and other written material can each make a difference.

Community Service

Admissions officers know that an altruistic student, one who has contributed to community life without regard for compensation, is more likely to contribute to campus life, be academically successful, and form a long-term attachment to the college or university. Therefore, volunteer activities should be documented in the application. One example is a talent in a particular sport in which the student participates competitively and coaches young children after school. In such a case, a letter of recommendation from the person who supervised the student's coaching should be in the applicant's folder. Another example might be contributing expertise in developing computer programs; the student may have shared this talent by writing programs that helped a social agency save some money. In this case, a letter of recommendation from the agency director or treasurer should be in the file.

Personal Recommendations

Students who are interested in selective or highly selective colleges will face a rigorous admission process. Each part of the application can make a difference when the admissions committee must decide between several highly qualified applicants. This includes personal recommendations that are well-written and effective. Effective recommendations answer the question, "What can you tell us about this student that will help us make a decision?" You should ask your counselors and teachers to provide evidence that distinguishes you from other equally qualified candidates and creates a complete and credible picture of you in the mind of an admissions officer.

- Ask for recommendations from teachers and others who know you well and are likely to take the time to write thoughtful comments.
- Ask for a recommendation from a teacher in the field in which you may wish to major, preferably a teacher who is genuinely interested in your future.
- Be sure to ask for recommendations well in advance (several weeks) of the deadline.
- Provide stamped envelopes that are preaddressed to the colleges.
- Thank the teacher. Inform him or her of the colleges' decisions.

In some cases, a recommendation can be used to explain quirks in the student's transcript. The following example illustrates this point.

Lisa was identified as gifted in elementary school. When she entered 9th grade, she was assigned to

153

rigorous courses and earned A's and B's. Her sophomore year yielded the same results. When Lisa reached 11th grade, teacher expectations changed. As a result, Lisa's midsemester grades in two academic courses were C and D. Lisa talked with her parents and decided to confront the problem with private tutoring and extra study. She also dropped out of some of her extracurricular activities. By the end of 11th grade, she earned B's in both subjects. When Lisa applied to selective colleges, her counselor wrote a recommendation that explained how Lisa overcame her problem. A teacher recommendation presented a picture of a highly gifted student who, when confronted with a problem, faced the situation realistically, set goals, and accomplished her mission.

Counselor Recommendations

Counselors who are responsible for more than 500 students would like to know each student well, but that's just not possible. If your guidance counselor does not know you well, make an appointment to discuss your college plans and goals. The following questions are just suggestions as to what information students can give their guidance counselor to use when writing a recommendation. This information may be helpful to your teachers, as well.

Counselor recommendations are most effective when they are specific and say what the student does that reflects his or her intellectual ability and growth; depth and breadth of extracurricular involvement; personal characteristics such as initiative, creativity, and leadership capacity; and generosity of spirit. Students, provide your counselors with answers to the following questions and ideas to help them write a recommendation letter for you.

Intellectual and Academic Development
1. To what extent have you taken advantage of academic choices available to you?

2. What course was the most difficult for you, and why? Why did you take that course?
3. How many nonrequired books do you read in a typical month? Year?
   - What type of nonrequired reading do you enjoy, and why?
   - Who is your favorite literary character, and why?

4. What else can you think of that has influenced your thinking?
   - a particular movie?
   - a cultural event?
   - an academic competition?
   - a particular teacher?
   - a particular mentor?
   - travel?
   - a summer experience?

5. Have you taken any academic courses that may not be listed on your transcript? When and where?
6. Are you involved in any artistic/creative activity or intellectual pursuit that is not reflected in your folder, and do you have samples of your work? For example, are you
   - a basement scientist?
   - a computer hacker?
   - a midnight poet?
   - a composer of music or song lyrics?
   - a puzzle creator?
   - a photographer?

Extracurricular Activities

155

1. List the extracurricular activities you have been involved in. Describe the length of time, depth, and breadth of your involvement. Can you rank your activities according to importance?
2. Have you received any prizes or honors?
3. What positions of leadership have you held?

a. Can you explain your methods of leadership?
b. How did you get results? Did you command? Cajole? Ask?
4. What have you gained from your extracurricular activity? How has it influenced your life?
5. Have you participated in any volunteer activity where you shared your talents? When and where did you volunteer? What did you do to share your talents?

Personal Information
1. Have you had to overcome any problems, difficulties, or disabilities? If so, how did you overcome the problem and what motivated you?
2. How much free time do you have each day and week, and how do you use your free time?
3. How hard have you had to work to achieve your accomplishments?
4. How academically prepared are you for college? How emotionally prepared? Do you feel prepared for the independence available on most college campuses?
5. What makes you unique, compared to your friends?
6. What do you see as the major problem in the United States today? In your state? In your high school? Can you make suggestions as to how to solve any of these problems?
7. What do you see yourself doing in 20 years? In 10 years? In 5 years? In 6 months?

Teacher Recommendations

Securing strong teacher recommendations is important, especially when the teacher can talk about your growth and development in an academic subject. Be sure to:

- Ask teachers and others well in advance, at least 2 or 3 weeks ahead of the deadline. Inform the person of the deadline.
- Ask teachers and others who know you well. If a person agrees to write a recommendation, make an appointment to explain your college plans.

- Provide teachers and others with stamped, addressed envelopes.
- Be sure to thank the person and keep him or her informed of the colleges' decisions.

The following guidelines may be helpful to give to your teachers when you ask for recommendations. The guidelines, as well as the sample recommendation that follows (see Figure 7), were contributed by a Virginia AP English teacher.

- Many colleges provide standard forms for evaluations. If you decide not to use a form, make sure that your letter of recommendation contains all the information requested.
- Teacher recommendations are most effective when they say what the student does that reflects his or her intellectual ability and growth, creativity, and generosity of spirit.
- Be specific. Support each statement with examples, descriptions of projects or presentations, and/or quotations from the student's writing.
- Use carefully thought-out language, avoiding clichés, stock phrases, overgeneralizations, ambiguities, and exaggerations that may diminish your future credibility.
- If the student has received an honor or award in your subject area, explain the nature and significance of the award.
- Keep in mind the student's choice of school and academic program.
- Some very selective colleges ask you to compare the student you are writing about with other students whom you have recommended in the past. Consider limiting the number of recommendations to such a school to two or three per year. You might suggest to the student that another teacher write the recommendation if yours, under the conditions of comparison, will be less favorable.

157

To Whom It May Concern:

Sara is, without doubt, one of the most brilliant students I have ever had the pleasure of knowing. What is so extraordinary about her career here at Anderson High School is not just her distinguished performance, but her mastery of a challenging curriculum 2 years ahead of her classmates. Such precocity is uncommon in the field of English.

In the 2 years that I have taught her, Sara has demonstrated an intellectual maturity belying her age. As an 11th grader, when she was 15 years old, she excelled in my Advanced Placement (12th grade) English class for the gifted and talented. During that year her writing developed swiftly and consistently. Always one to seek the most difficult challenge, Sara wrote critical essays on works by authors such as William Faulkner and Thomas Mann with an understanding and expressiveness that touched the core of her subjects. Like a true writer, she drives herself, revising and polishing, always measuring her own achievement against that of the best writers—professional novelists, critics, and lately, poets. Sara frequently questions her own abilities, but, happily, this questioning leads her to new levels of artistic and intellectual activity. Her internal urge for perfection, her keen sense of form, and her unfailing imagination have enabled her to produce outstanding works in both literary analysis and fiction. Sara's short story, "The Tenth Tape," appeared in last year's literary arts magazine. One of my colleagues, having read the story, found it to be as absorbing as a "real story by an adult." It came as no surprise that Sara received the highest score (5) on the AP English examination.

This year Sara is my student in an independent study course, one that I designed especially for her as a sequel to the AP English course. It is exciting to participate in her continuous growth as an intellect and scholar. Thriving in an environment that allows her to set her own challenges, she pursues ideas with a rigor and scholarship that are enviable. In her most recent essay, on Virginia Woolf's *The Waves*, for example, she has presented a powerfully persuasive argument against critic James Naremore's contention that the work is a failure, stifling in effect, and almost drowning the reader in language. Sara develops a countercriticism suggesting that, to the contrary, Woolf's language corresponds organically to the point she is making.

In my creative writing course, which Sara is taking as an elective, she seems to have discovered "her own voice." Her narra-

Figure 7. Sample teacher recommendation

tives, in unaffected, rhythmic prose, engage the reader and spark the imagination; her dialogues resonate with the natural sounds of speech. She can be intensely moving without any hint of sentimentality. Her artist's ear for sound and language has led her, perhaps inevitably, to write poetry. Sara's poems are impressive in their originality and craftsmanship. She has excellent control over rhythm and imagery, weaving lines like the following (from the middle of a surrealistic poem still in the draft stage):

> Mr. McGuire smiles at me/I see in his wide wet mouth/ the spaces where his teeth once were/and try to run./My feet are caught in the vines, stuck/in thorny loops, and the cucumbers bulge/ like popping green fish-eyes/turning toward me in the wind ...

Despite the effort Sara puts into her creative and scholarly work, she still finds time to help others (she is the ideal student tutor: gentle, patient, and often funny) and to participate in extracurricular activities. She is an invaluable member of the English Team, the layout editor of the school newspaper, and the literary editor of the literary arts magazine, for which I am the adviser. We all enjoy working with Sara and know we can always count on her good judgment and imagination.

Sara is a wonderful combination of ingenuousness and brilliance. I admire her integrity, self-discipline, and generosity of spirit. She has my highest recommendation for admission to your university.

Signature
Title

Figure 7. Sample teacher recommendation, continued

The College Interview

Most students waste the interview—they don't prepare. They walk into my office and wait for something to happen. For these students, the interview is not a selection factor.

—Dean of Admissions, small public university

You need to learn how to use the interview to your advantage. The standard advice offered by well-intentioned people

159

is "Be yourself," but that is much too general for gifted students; they think of too many alternatives. Gifted students may deal with general advice by focusing on one factor, such as how to dress for the interview, and then respond by swinging from one extreme to another. Some students will arrive in a sweatshirt and ragged jeans, others in a brand new suit or dress. In either case, you may be out of character and feel and look quite uncomfortable.

Prior to an interview, you can review and discuss the list of questions presented later in this chapter. An interview practice session in which you and a classmate role-play an admissions officer and an applicant is an ideal way to demonstrate this part of the application process. You should decide which questions are important; however, you should be aware that highly selective colleges value certain questions. The factors that are important to you will determine the degree to which the college interview provides information that results in a match. For example, you may ask, "What are the most recent experiences your college has had in placing graduates in jobs, professional schools, or graduate schools?" If an admissions officer values that type of question and provides an adequate answer (one that goes beyond information provided in the guides), you will acquire valuable information and the admissions officer will have insight into what you want from a college.

Students, you should check to see whether on-campus interviews are offered. Many colleges now ask local alumni to conduct interviews; in this case, the local interviewer will contact you after your application is received.

Guidelines for an effective interview are presented shortly, but you should never "program" yourself to ask specific questions or answer questions in a specific way. Admissions officers recognize and value spontaneity. Consider, for example, the following two actual cases.

During an interview, Kara noticed that her interviewer had a partially completed crossword puzzle on her desk. Kara mentioned the puzzle, and a conversation about their shared passion for puzzles followed. Kara recommended that the admissions officer subscribe to *Games* magazine. When she returned home, Kara wrote a thank-you note to the admissions officer, asking whether she had sent in a subscription to *Games* magazine.

Following an interview during which it snowed heavily, Terrance found that his car was snowed in and immovable. He returned to the admissions office, where he and the admissions officer had a brief, humorous discussion about unexpected snowfalls. Terrance and the admissions officer solved the problem by convincing a campus security officer to help get the car to a relatively passable road. Following the interview he wrote a thank-you note to the admissions officer and added that he now carried a shovel and sand in his car to help him get out of snowdrifts.

Most of the suggestions listed in the guidelines that follow are general in nature. However, counselors can assign groups of students to rehearse scenarios in which the principles for specific colleges are followed. Guidelines for an effective interview include:

- Approach the interview with this in mind: You are about to invest thousands of dollars and 4 years of your life in an institution that may shape your values and career plans. What can you do during an interview to help you make the best decision about that investment and your future? If you do decide to invest in that institution, what information can you provide that will convince them to accept your application?
- If you are really interested in a selective college, research the institution thoroughly. Approach the interview as an opportunity to share information. Be prepared to say that you are interested and give reasons.
- Construct an agenda that asks questions that cannot be answered by reading college catalogs. For example, ask what percentage of the freshman class returns for sophomore year, or, if many students do not return, ask

161

whether the college knows why. Do not ask how many books are in the library. There are more than you can read.

- Construct an agenda that will answer the personal question "What does this institution offer that will help me reach my goals?"
- Answer the interviewer's questions honestly. Prepare and rehearse, but don't overprogram yourself.
- Be prepared to present information about yourself that is not visible in your written application and supporting material. Remember, the admissions committee is struggling to decide, "Which of these highly qualified applicants shall we admit, and which must we deny?"
- Write down your interviewer's name; write a thank-you note as soon as you return home.

Remember, the interview is a time for colleges to evaluate you and determine whether you may be a better candidate than someone else for their school. Some questions you may be asked in the interview include the following:

- Why do you want to go to this college?
- What do you want to know about this college?
- What have you read lately?
- Are there any particular subjects or authors you enjoy?
- How did you spend last summer?
- What has been important to you in high school?
- What do you consider to be your major strength? Weakness?
- Do you know what area you want to concentrate on in college? Why did you choose this particular area?
- During your free time at this school, in what activities might you participate?

Asking questions of the school representative during the interview may help you make your decision about whether or not you want to attend that college. Some questions you may want to ask during the interview include:

- What do you consider to be your outstanding departments?

- Can you take courses for credit in areas such as music or art if you are not going to major in them?
- At a university with a graduate school, you might want to ask: If I were in a preprofessional program here at your school, would it improve my chances of being admitted to your graduate school?
- Are there any opportunities to work on campus?
- Do you have an honor system (for student conduct and issues such as cheating) here? Are faculty members and students satisfied that everyone respects the honor system, especially during final examinations?

The College Application Essay

The essay is the bane of every high school senior's college application. Some students refuse to consider colleges where they might be extremely happy because an essay is required. Some students write their essays the night before the deadline; others spend weeks writing and rewriting. Only the college application deadline puts an end to the agony. If you have prior experience in writing, you will find that writing an autobiographical essay is a growth-promoting experience—after you overcome the anxiety produced by a series of open-ended, sometimes deceptively challenging questions such as "Tell us something about yourself that is not reflected in your application folder" or "Discuss your academic and professional goals."

You may have earned straight A's in a highly rigorous academic program, have earned more than adequate SAT or ACT scores, and have a social conscience and participate in many community activities, but still feel uneasy at the thought of outlining your academic and professional goals. How do you "evaluate a personal or educational experience" that has been "a major factor" in your getting old enough to apply to college? Given the age of most high school seniors, it is not surprising that some feel uncomfortable. You may wonder, "What does this question have to do with my ability

163

to succeed in and contribute to that school?" The more competitive colleges, however, require essays, detailed written analyses of extracurricular activities, and/or personal statements. They are asking the question, "Who are you?" You should answer all questions, but in particular you should focus on the one that reads "What can you tell us about yourself that we have not asked?" If you take the time to write an effective answer to such a question, it may make the difference between acceptance and rejection.

Personal essays and statements should answer the question "Who are you?" from your perspective. The essay is your opportunity to take control. Questions reflect the college; responses reflect the student. Essays should answer the question that was asked and say something about your ability to organize, reflect, and write clearly. A well-written essay can make an applicant come alive on paper so that the reader can recognize her as a match for the college. If the essay is to make a significant difference to an admissions officer, you need to be aware of your strengths and limitations, and write reflectively.

The essay can be a decisive factor. It can reassure the admissions committee that you are capable of college-level work. Teachers, counselors, and parents may review your essays for spelling and grammar mistakes, but not the essay topic. Of course, admissions staff read essays differently—we all have our own reading style—but in general, they are looking for qualities they believe are important. What are they looking for? Evidence of writing ability, intellectual curiosity, initiative and motivation, creativity, self-discipline, character, capacity for growth, leadership potential, and community service. Consistency with other elements of your application also is very important. For example, if you claim to have strong leadership skills but do not hold a leadership position in any activities, that shows an inconsistency between your essay and your application.

The following prompts are several sample essay questions for the college application.

- Students are asked to deal with a 2" x 4" rectangle on a blank piece of paper. The directions say, "Do something creative

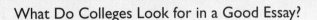

What Do Colleges Look for in a Good Essay?

- Writing ability

- Intellectual curiosity

- Initiative and motivation

- Creativity

- Self-discipline

- Character

- Capacity for growth

- Leadership potential

- Community service

- Consistency with other elements of the student's application

in this space. We are interested not only in your academic credentials, but also in your imagination and creativity."

- Students are asked to "do something" with an 11″ x 13″ piece of paper.

- You have just completed a 300-page autobiography. Please submit page 261.

- You are a journalist with the rare opportunity to interview any person—living, deceased, or fictional. Whom would you choose? What do you feel you could learn from this person? Answer in 300 to 500 words.

- Describe an experience that has altered or profoundly affected your present life or intended goals. The experience may be an accident, a competition, or anything of great significance to you.

- Make up a question, state it clearly, and answer it.

Guidelines for Writing a College Application Essay

The following is a step-by-step process that may help students practice and produce a better essay.

1. Write several short essays. Write about what you do in school and what you do outside of school. (If you are an 11th-grade student, consider keeping a journal so that you will have many writing samples by application time.) Be specific. For example, you might write about:
   - Your most important learning experience.
   - Your favorite academic class and/or teacher.
   - The rise and fall of your science fair project.
   - The trials and rewards of your work on a school publication.
   - Your selection as captain of the football team.
   - Your lack of athletic prowess.
   - Your work as a clerk at a discount store.
   - Your experience in a fast-food emporium.
   - A volunteer experience.

2. Try to write about yourself in at least three different settings so that you can see yourself from several angles. List all of the adjectives you would use to describe yourself in each of these settings.

3. Define your characteristics. Ask yourself:
   - What outstanding characteristic or cluster of characteristics crop up in my writings?
   - Am I dependable, with good work habits?
   - Am I creative, with a good sense of humor?
   - Am I a person of contradictions? (Many of us are.)

4. Examine the question you are expected to answer.
   - Decide exactly what the question asks. You may want to check with your family or counselor because misinterpreting the question is a common mistake.
   - Decide which characteristics should be included in your answer.

- Decide which example or examples should be included in your answer.

5. Write your answer.
6. Examine your answer. Try answering the following questions:
   - Did my essay really answer the question? Am I the only person who could have written this essay? (If the answer is no, you need to examine ways to make your essay more reflective of you.)
   - Does this essay include concrete examples to illustrate my points? (If the answer is no, you need to examine ways to include specific examples and illustrations.)
   - Is this essay an interesting enough answer to the question that a reader will be able to concentrate on it after reading many other essays? (If the answer is no, you need to examine ways to help the reader remain interested.) Caution: Make your essay interesting, as opposed to strange and bizarre. For example, change the pacing and relate abstract concepts to concrete examples.

7. Revise your answer. Rewrite, rewrite, rewrite. You may need several revisions before you have an interesting essay that uses concrete examples and is self-reflective.
8. Edit your answer, checking grammar, spelling, and punctuation.
9. Type your essay. You do not want a tired admissions officer to attempt to read your handwriting at midnight after she has read hundreds of essays.
10. Mail your application.
11. Permit yourself one long sigh of relief!

167

Sample Student Essays

Essay questions vary from school to school and year to year. Highly selective schools generally phrase essay questions to encourage an applicant to write autobiographical-ly—to describe something about himself that is not obvious in the application and supporting material. The following samples were written by applicants to highly selective or selective universities in response to some general questions. Notice that they answer the question, as well as identify the student as both a problem finder and a problem solver.

Question: What can you tell us about yourself that is not revealed in your application?

Student answer:

> What is God?
> Is He mod?
> Is He of the old sod?
> Does He have a bod?
> Is He British or bluish or Jewish
> Or Venusian?
> Excuse-He-can all my sins.
> Is He big-time on cloud nine or bovine
> Or from Constantinople?
> I-hope-He'll still let me in.
> Hey, what's that storm brewing?
> Doesn't He like what I'm doing?
> What fate does He have stewing?
> Is that lightning?
> Oh crap.
> Zap!

Slumping Senior

I am the slumping senior, I'm here to sing my song.
I've worked real hard the past 12 years but I've been in school too long.
I don't want all the pressure, but I know it's just be-gun.
If I had my way I'd skip every day,
I'd sleep till ten and then be with my friends
And we could all go have some fun.

I am the slumping senior, I'm way too far behind.
If I get one more assignment, I think I'll lose my mind.
I've got an English paper, I've got a physics test;
I know it's true, tomorrow they're due,
I know it's late, if I start at eight
By four I'll get some rest.
I am the slumping senior, I've thought the whole thing through.
School won't really matter much when I'm thirty-two.
I've learned to play the game of life, I think I'm doing fine
Cause all the trends and all my friends
Are the only things worth remembering
When it's ten years down the line.

I consider myself to be a "math" person. Problem solving in mathematics requires the application of definite processes to determine an answer that is either correct or incorrect. English is completely different; however, poetry provides a middle ground, which I thoroughly enjoy. Rhyme and rhythm give a poem a set pattern that I can follow easily, and the change of just one word can make the poem "correct" or "incorrect." My poems are always humorous, but vary from the outrageous "What is God?" to the autobiographical "Slumping Senior."

Question: What activity have you participated in that has influenced you the most?

Student answer:

In the summer of ____, I had an experience that taught me more about myself than any other event in my life. I participated in a three-week multi-element Outward Bound course in North Carolina consisting of rock climbing, canoeing, and hiking. Throughout the course I learned the importance of teamwork, commitment to achieving my goals, and the qualities of leadership. I will always reflect back on that unique experience as a time in my life when I learned so much that shaped my values, attitudes, and personality.

The most memorable experience I had there was rock climbing. I had never been so scared before in my life. Hundreds of feet up in the air I held onto the face of a cliff by a metal clasp. Once I overcame my fear of falling I had to concentrate on climbing up the face. Many times I came to a dead end; I didn't quit, but only after I gained some confidence in myself would I find safety at the next ledge. From this experience I learned to trust myself and push the limit of my abilities. When I get stuck on something I know I will keep trying new ways until I come up with the right one that works for me. I believe that this lesson I learned will help me accomplish difficult tasks in college. I will not give up when things get tough because I know how it feels to achieve something for which I have struggled.

I learned teamwork in the canoeing part of the course. When two people are in a canoe together it is crucial that they work together if they want to accomplish anything. I learned this lesson the hard way, only after smashing into submerged boulders and capsizing into roaring rapids did I realize that I couldn't do everything on my own. This lesson of teamwork will help me in college because I know now that I have to work together with faculty and other students to get the best possible education.

Another experience I had of pushing my limits was the last event of the course, a 14-mile marathon. The choice was given to us to run 9 or 14 miles. I chose the 14 miles because I didn't know if I could do it or not and I wanted to know what my limits were. It felt so good to finish that race, knowing that I accomplished something that I didn't know if I could do. I find it amazing how people can always perform past what they believe to be their limits. I will always remember this experience because whenever I come to a problem in my life I know I won't take the easy way out.

The most grueling part of the course was hiking. We had to carry all our food, equipment, and clothes in our packs and had to hike up and down hills for long periods of time without rest. Through this part of the course I learned that I do have leadership qualities. I put a lot of effort into finding trails, organizing campsites, and taking charge of expeditions. On one occasion, when we had lost the trail and the rest of the group had given up, I made a very determined effort to find the trail and led the group to our destination. From this experience I found that I don't like to sit back and let other people do things for me. I like to make things happen for myself, to create opportunities. This enthusiasm and creativity will help me excel in college.

These experiences will always be memorable to me because they have helped me discover what kind of person I am. The values and attitudes I have developed from these experiences will help me with my future in college and my life.

Question: In an essay of no more than 300 words, explain how you feel that engineering and applied science can best benefit humanity in the next decade.

Student Answer:

The science of engineering always involves the recognition of a problem and the determination to solve it. The size of the problem is irrelevant. It can vary from something as small as the configuration of a paper clip to something as large as putting a man on the moon. The method of solving the problem is the same. It involves proposing possible solutions within a set scientific procedure.

171

Engineering is an integral part of human progress. Without it there would be no answers or solutions to the challenges man has faced through the centuries. It is easy to see how far mankind has come and, at the same time, to see that we have just begun to develop. I think the next decade will involve the need for thinkers and planners trained in engineering. We are on the verge of discovering many exciting solutions, including the cures for many diseases and the establishment of a space station. Discoveries in space for aerospace engineers are just as important as a cure for cancer is for the biomedical engineer. Some may think the latter is more important. It may be, but the dreams of the engineers and the challenges they face in finding solutions are the same. That is the important part. It is hard to predict the future and to know what particular discovery will be more beneficial than another, but one thing is clear: without a group of well-trained engineers, those discoveries won't be made.

It can be said that engineering is one of the oldest professions. It hasn't always been called engineering, of course, but there have always been people who have looked for answers within an engineering framework. That is how man has progressed scientifically. As we head into the next century, engineers will be ready to raise questions and propose solutions.

Tipping the Balance

Each year, colleges have to select their freshman class from a host of qualified students. It is important to look at some of the more subtle factors that are considered and that can tip the balance in favor of admission when a college is making up the freshman class.

- What does the school need, and are you uniquely qualified to fill that need? Special or unique qualities that you will bring to a college community can tip the balance your favor.

- Would you contribute diversity to the campus? Although colleges are not permitted to decide admissions solely on the basis of race or culture, campus diversity is highly valued. Your ethnic origins may tip the balance in your favor.
- Are you a legacy or does your family have an educational history at this school? A legacy means "something handed down." In the case of college admissions, it literally means that admission is handed down from the parent alumnus. If either of your parents attended a university where you have applied, that makes you a legacy. If you do not have the academic record required by that college, it won't make a difference. But, in a tough competition where you need an edge, being a legacy can tip the balance in your favor.

Decisions: The College Envelope Arrives, Now What?

If your application for admission has been accepted by more than one school—and if you followed the process outlined in this book and chose wisely, that will surely happen—how are you going to decide which college you should attend?

- Revisit the schools that seriously interest you. Colleges often look different than they did when you were "just looking." Try to arrange an overnight stay in the dorms, sit in on a freshman class, eat several meals, and visit the library.
- Eating in all venues will give you an idea as to what to expect. If you hate the food that a school offers, or if there is no salad bar and you are a vegan, realize that you will have to eat off-campus most of the time, and that can add hundreds of dollars to your education expenses.

- Look again at what you wanted from a school when you used the questionnaire in this book. Is that fascinating professor going to teach freshmen or do teaching assistants teach his or her classes? Are the professors friendly?
- Check out college nightlife. Nightlife may seem like a trivial consideration; after all, this is college, it's supposed to be about education. It is largely about education, but it's hard to spend 4 years accomplishing your academic goals if you hate your life because there's nothing to do. Having fun is one of the keys to staying sane.
- Talk to people. If an alumnus interviewed you, talk to that person about campus life. Talk to students. Go to the Web site and see if there are Weblogs that will give you a sense of what it's like to be a student at that school.

Waiting Lists

In 2004, 57% of all wait-listed students opted to remain on the wait list. An average of 27% of all students who were placed on the wait list ultimately gained admission to the college or university that wait-listed them (NACAC, 2004a).

What happens if you are placed on the waiting list of a school you really want to attend? There are several things you can do.

- First, ensure your place at a school that accepted your application by sending a deposit.
- Find out what being on the waiting list means at the particular college. That is, ask how many students they usually accept from the waiting list, and if they rank students on the waiting list. According to the National Association for College Admission Counseling (Gross, 2002), about one third of colleges and universities use wait lists, and a student's chances of admission is about one in five. These are general numbers and subject to change each year.
- Ask your guidance counselor to find out why you were placed on the waiting list. The reasons will help determine the best action to take. For example, if your folder

indicates specific weaknesses, you may be able to submit substantive additional information that will influence the dean or director of admissions.

- If the college considers you a "viable" candidate, or one who will be accepted if a vacancy develops, ask your guidance counselor to lobby actively for you.
- Write to the dean of admissions, indicate your intent to attend the school, and ask him or her to review your folder. State your reasons for requesting that your application be reviewed.
- Consider other influences you can bring to bear on the matter. You may know alumni who will support your admission to the school. Be careful, however, of overkill.
- Find out the projected schedule for admitting students on the waiting list. Ask when you can expect to hear from the college. It may not happen until August, so you have to decide how badly you want to attend that school.
- Apply elsewhere. Some colleges have nontraditional admission. That is, they admit students during the winter break before the second semester. Or, you might enter a school on probation, in which case it's up to you to prove you can do the work.
- Consider attending your second-choice college or university for a year. You may have a better chance as a transfer applicant than as a graduating high school senior, if you can prove that you are capable of high achievement.

What if you are rejected by all of the colleges you applied to? Do not despair. Ask your guidance counselor to find out the reason for each rejection. Compare the reasons. Is there a pattern or central theme? The answers to some of the following questions will determine your action:

- Were *all* the schools flooded with applicants this year?
- Was there some confusion regarding the presentation of information in your application?
- Did you have a specific academic weakness?

If there is no central theme, perhaps you miscalculated your options. For example, did you apply to a range of

175

schools that included at least one that you knew would accept your application and several whose admission requirements matched your credentials? Each summer, the NACAC keeps a list of schools that have vacancies and would welcome additional applicants. Ask your counselor about the list, or check the NACAC Web site.

The following are some possibilities for strengthening your chances at a later time:

- Look at other colleges with similar characteristics.
- Submit additional applications to colleges with rolling or late admissions policies.
- After June 1, inquire about unanticipated openings. (This is called "summer meltdown.")
- Spend a year investigating career paths: Find an internship, work in a law office, or volunteer for a community service project.
- Spend a year bolstering your academic weaknesses: Take some courses at a local community college to prove you can do college-level work.
- Look for a sense of direction and begin again!

College Costs

This section is a general overview of college costs to help families be more resourceful in meeting the college cost needs of their students. However, college cost information changes yearly, and the needs of gifted students vary widely. For current detailed information, consult the publications *The A's and B's of Academic Scholarships* (Leider, 2005), *College.edu* (Guernsey, 2005), and *Don't Miss Out: The Ambitious Student's Guide to Financial Aid* (Leider & Leider, 2005). More information about college costs is available online at http://www.thinktuition.com.

The Bad News

Educating a gifted student after high school is not a one-shot, 1-year affair. Gifted students often invest heavily in both time and college costs in post-high-school education. Think of it in terms of 2 years for an associate degree, 4 years for a bachelor's, 6 years or longer for a graduate or professional degree, and even longer if there are younger brothers or sisters spaced 2 or 4 years apart. You and your family may pay college bills for many years following high school graduation, so it is important to understand the overall costs of college.

What stands out immediately is cause for concern. Each year the cost of a college education and our ability to pay it are reassessed by a federally approved system called *need analysis*. If current trends continue, costs will continue to outpace inflation. If tuition increases at twice the present inflation rate (3.2%), a $12,000 tuition bill in a student's freshman year will be a $20,000 tuition bill 4 years later.

There are several reasons why tuition and other college costs continue to rise. First, higher education is labor intensive. Great teaching comes from conversation and discussion among inquiring minds. But, faculty salaries are comparatively low, so catch-up raises are necessary to attract new professors and keep tenured faculty members from leaving academia for higher incomes in the corporate world.

Second, state support for higher education is lagging behind increased cost. Public universities, as well as community colleges, depend on state appropriations for more than half their support. When appropriations fail to match rising costs, colleges must compensate by raising in-state tuition and sharply raising tuition for out-of-state students.

The third factor is technology. To provide high-quality education, colleges need to spend money for up-to-date laboratories, research equipment, and wireless campuses, as well as the supporting maintenance and training staffs.

Finally, with few exceptions, colleges can no longer meet the financial needs of all students. One solution is to raise tuition rates by two to three times the rate of inflation. Students who can afford the increases are, in effect, helping to subsidize those who need financial aid.

In addition to the news that tuition will continue to outpace inflation, a second bit of bad news is that federal student aid continues in a lean cycle. Although the dollar amount of federal grants and loans increases each school year, new programs are being added and other programs are being stretched to help reduce the federal budget deficit.

Of equal concern is the unstable delivery of federal student aid. In order to add, cut, or stretch some programs, the associated timetables, eligibility rules, interest rates, and even student aid forms have changed from year to year. These changes will continue in magnitude and frequency. The result is confused students, parents, and guidance counselors and extremely overworked college financial aid personnel.

The Good News

The flip side of the coin is that if you are fortunate enough not to need assistance in meeting your college costs, you have a better chance of being accepted by the college to which you apply.

Most colleges must compete for good students. This competition for the right student translates into recruiting drives, alumni interviews, special honors programs, and scholarships designed to attract the brightest available students. The more marketable the student—good ACT/SAT scores, grade point average, and class standing, together with leadership, athletic ability, or talent—the more nonfederal, college-sponsored student financial assistance there is to help defray college costs. You and your parents need to make wise choices when selecting a college.

Getting Your Fair Share

Before you reach for a share of these extra dollars, you need to understand what makes up the student's part of college costs, namely the cost of attendance. The cost of attendance consists of six separate items: tuition, room, board, books, transportation, and miscellaneous expenses. Miscellaneous expenses include insurance and laundry costs, telephone bills, and even the cost of the trips to the local fast food restaurant when what the dining hall features does not appeal to you.

The cost of attendance is different for each student, even for students at the same college. Some students live in dormitories, others in off-campus housing, and others at home with their parents. The cost of travel or commuting varies depending upon circumstances, as do special expenses associated with disabilities, age, and family or child care.

The most expensive private college in the United States costs more than $45,000 per year for tuition, room, and board. The cost of 4 years at an Ivy-League school is about $180,000. Depending on whether you are an in-state or out-of-state student, 4 years at a public institution can range from $48,000 to $100,000.

A student can normally receive assistance in meeting college costs if the calculated *family contribution* is lower than the cost of attendance. The difference between the two is the *financial need.*

Financial need is simply a number; it does not necessarily mean that your family is poor. It does mean that you may qualify for student aid in order to attend the college of your choice. For example, Alex's family is able to contribute $12,000 per year to his college costs. He is considering three universities: Ivy X, at about $45,000 per year; Midrange U, at about $33,000; and Home State U, which will cost about $12,000. Alex's family has calculated their financial need and the amount they would qualify for in student aid. At Ivy X they would qualify for $35,000 to help with the annual cost, at Midrange U they would qualify for $21,000 in aid, and at Home State U there would be no financial need at all.

Understanding Family Contributions

The amount of money a family is able to contribute to college costs is the key to estimating the amount of financial aid for which they will qualify. The family contribution is essentially the sum of four separate calculations: the contribution from the parents' income, the contribution from the parents' assets, the contribution from the student's income, and the contribution from the student's assets (Berkner, Berker, Rooney, & Peter, 2003; Berkner et al., 2005).

179

Parental income includes the total of all taxable and non-taxable income. A family maintenance allowance is subtracted from this total. The larger the family, the larger the allowance. Income and social security taxes are also subtracted. The remainder is referred to as discretionary income. Depending on the amount, a percentage is taken and the result is considered the parents' contribution from income.

The next calculation is a percentage of the value of the parents' assets. The total value of savings, stocks, bonds, trust funds, mutual funds, money market funds, commodities, land and mortgage contracts held, and business and farm assets is calculated when considering eligibility for federal assistance. An asset protection allowance for retirement is subtracted based on the age of the oldest parent. Approximately 5.6% of the remainder is added to the family contribution. You can expect a private institution to add home equity to the list before they will use any of their scarce resources to assist a student.

Next, the student receives a $2,440 after-tax income protection allowance. Fifty percent of income over the allowance is added to the family contribution. Finally, the student's assets are evaluated. No asset protection allowance is permitted, because the student is considered to have a full working life ahead of him or her. The formula adds 35% of the student's assets to the family contribution (Berkner et al., 2003).

The sum of these four calculations, the family contribution to college cost, is what the student is expected to pay for his or her college education. The family contribution subtracted from the cost for a particular college determines the amount of student financial need and the amount of student aid for the school year. The calculation is recomputed each school year.

Multistudent Families. What happens if there is more than one member of a family in college at the same time? How does the family contribution to college cost change? In this common situation, a separate family contribution is calculated for each student, consisting of the parents' contribution from income and assets. For example, suppose that the total parental contribution is $12,000 and there are two students. Then $6,000 is allocated to each student. Son Jason's contribution from earnings and assets is $1,500, while daughter Gina's is $2,000. Consequently, the family contribution for Jason's college cost will be $7,500, and for Gina's will be $8,000.

Divorced or Separated Parents. Which parent's income and assets are used in the calculation when parents are divorced or separated? The answer depends upon which parent the student lived with for the greater portion of the calendar year preceding the year the student enters college. If the custodial parent has remarried, stepparent income and assets are included. Also, a student facing this situation and seeking nonfederal college financial assistance should be aware that most private colleges will likely ask the other natural parent to submit a divorced-parent financial form before awarding any financial assistance.

Filling Out the Forms

How do colleges get the information they need to calculate the family contribution to college cost? As soon as possible after the first of the year, the student and his or her family should fill out a need-analysis form called the FAFSA. Students applying for early selection must do this twice, first when they apply, and again after the first of the year.

A student seeking to determine whether he or she qualifies for some of the college's own money or money from the state in which the student resides in addition to federal financial aid, may be required to fill out the College Board's CSS Profile or the American College Testing Program's family financial statement. Both forms require a processing fee. Information about these forms is normally obtained from high school guidance offices and college financial aid offices. Some colleges have unique financial aid forms attached to the admission application.

Putting Scholarships to Work

Most people believe that receipt of a scholarship reduces their family contribution to college costs. However, while the scholarship may help pay the college bill, it may not reduce the student's or the family's share of the bill.

For example, the Johnson family contribution was determined to be $9,000. At her high school commencement, her town civic association awarded Sally Johnson a $1,000 scholarship. The Johnsons were elated, thinking that their family contribution would now be $8,000. Unfortunately, they were wrong: The contribution remained the same. By law, Sally's college just took the amount of the scholarship and incorporated it into Sally's student aid package.

This does not mean that students heading for college should stop looking for and working toward scholarships and grants. Rather, they should concentrate their efforts on seeking scholarships large enough to cover both the family contribution and the student aid award. The best advice is not to waste time seeking special scholarships or seeking out computerized scholarship services that charge a fee for their work. Saving money for college is a better course of action. Some scholarship money goes unused each year, but it is primarily unused employee tuition benefits, not scholarships for which no one has applied.

Financial Aid in Return for Service in the Military or Other Government Programs

Persons serving in all branches of the U.S. Armed Forces on active duty or in the Reserves, or those participating in a Reserve Officer Training Corps (R.O.T. C.) program while attending college, can earn entitlements that may cover up to 100% of college tuition, fees and books, plus additional dollars for expenses. In addition, a variety of federal government programs such as AmeriCorps and others at the state level offer funds for college tuition for those who volunteer and complete their terms of service.

182

More About Money

In the 2003-2004 academic year, the latest year for which statistics are available, about 16.5 million undergraduates were enrolled in postsecondary institutions for all or part of the year as full- or part-time students. Twenty-seven percent of all undergraduates enrolled in public 4-year institutions in 2003–2004 received a federal grant (e.g., Pell), 21% received institutional grants, 19% received state grants, and 14% received grants from other sources such as employers or private organizations. The average federal grant amount was $2,800, the average institutional grant was $2,900, the average state grant was $2,200, and the average grant funded through other sources was $2,000 (Berkner et al., 2005; Leider & Leider, 2005).

According to the College Board (n.d.d), the average comprehensive tuition rate for public ($11,376) and private colleges ($27,485) is significantly higher than the mean federal grant disbursed per student. On average, the institutions with the highest tuition are private institutions with small enrollments, institutions that are highly selective, and those that have low yield rates. Private colleges and colleges with low enrollments also have a slightly larger percentage of students receiving federal grant aid than public schools and those with high enrollments. Dependent need-based aid is provided to students based on their family income and their need for financial assistance. Non-need-based state aid, including merit aid, has continued to grow over the last 10 years. Non-need-based aid is awarded to students based on factors not pertaining to income, such as high academic achievement. Currently, 77% of state financial aid is distributed through need-based aid, and 23% through non-need-based aid (Leider, 2005; Leider & Leider, 2005).

Next to buying a home and paying for retirement, the cost of sending children to college is the largest financial challenge most parents face. If you wait until your children are in high school before saving, when your child graduates from high school you probably won't have enough to pay for 4 years of college. So, do some research, start saving early, and be consistent in depositing money into whatever type of account you choose. Here are five ways to save money for college (Willis, 2005):

1. Coverdell Education Savings Account (ESA) plans are similar to Individual Retirement Accounts (IRA)

183

in that they are tax-sheltered investment accounts available to U.S. taxpayers who deposit up to a maximum of $2,000 per year that will be used for college (Savingforcollege.com, n.d.a). Savings are tax deferred. If more than one person is depositing to a child's account, care must be taken that the total does not exceed the limit—$2,000. If the contribution is not used for education, eventually the funds will revert back to the student. You can't just refund the account back to yourself.

2. 529 accounts are education savings plans operated by a state or educational institution designed to help families set aside funds for future college costs. The plans are named after Section 529 of the Internal Revenue Code. There are 92 separate state 529 plans that vary widely and there are some national plans for those who move frequently. There is no annual contribution limit, as there is with the ESA. Savings are tax-deferred for a limited number of years (Savingforcollege.com, n.d.b). These plans may be accompanied by hefty fees, so look carefully before you jump into one. Do your homework and talk to a financial planner to compare the plans and look at how well they perform over time.

What happens if the 529 account beneficiary doesn't go to college? You can transfer the account to another college-bound beneficiary, as long as he or she is an eligible family member. If you don't use a 529 account for eligible expenses, earnings on your withdrawals are taxable and usually subject to a penalty.

3. Prepaid state tuition plans allow you to save money by paying for college now, but only if your teen will attend a state school. It may sound good, but prepaid tuition plans reduce financial aid eligibility.

4. Education savings bonds are a risk-free investment, but there is a limit on exemptions if your adjusted gross income is too high. The money is held in the parent's name, which can be a good thing, because the child isn't penalized when applying for financial aid.

5. Large corporations like McDonald's or Staples, and more than 40,000 retail stores, 7,000 restaurants, 10,000 hotels, and 350 online retailers will give you college contributions through the Upromise rebate program (see http://www.upromise.com). The Upromise Web site describes the program as a "free rebating program that helps families save money for college." Major companies where you can get rebates include America Online, Avis, and Borders Books & Music.

Some Final Words

The matter of paying college costs should not be taken lightly. A parent should not "let Johnny worry about it," any more than Johnny should "let Mom and Dad worry about it." The entire family needs to get involved.

Paying college costs requires research, study, and analysis. It should be discussed with high school counselors and college financial aid personnel, who have special knowledge of personal financial matters—loans, interest rates, tax laws, and innovative tuition payment plans. Knowing as much as possible about college costs can save time and money. What is most important is to know and understand the details about the entire spectrum of financing a gifted student's college education *before* filling out the first financial assistance form.

College Planning Glossary and Glossary of Financial Terms

Academic performance: the combination of a student's grade point average (GPA), class rank, transcript, standardized test scores, evidence of academic rigor, and other available numerical information. Some large schools consider a student's high school academic performance record the only criterion for an offer of admission.

Academic rigor: the relative difficulty of an academic course and the relative difficulty of all courses taken by a student during high school. Highly selective colleges expect a student to take the most rigorous curriculum offered.

Advanced Placement (AP) Examinations: exams offered each May by participating schools to students who want to be tested at the college level in many areas, including English, calculus, science, foreign languages, and music. Enrollment in an AP course is not required, and a fee is charged for each examination. AP tests are scored 1 to 5, with 5 being the highest score. Grades of 3, 4, or 5 on AP Examinations may be considered acceptable for college credit or exemption from required courses. Each college or university decides how much credit will be awarded to the student, and highly selective schools may give credit only for a 5. If a student takes an AP test, the student is responsible for ensuring that the score reaches the college.

Advanced Placement (AP) Program: program sponsored by the College Entrance Examination Board consisting of rigorous academic courses and examinations in 15 subjects. AP courses provide an opportunity for students to pursue college-level studies while still enrolled in secondary school, and demonstrate the student's capacity to handle college-level work. A high grade in an AP course is considered evidence of superior ability, even if a student doesn't take the AP test.

ACT assessment test: a content-oriented test, divided into four subject areas—math, science, English, and social studies—and an optional writing section. Scores are reported on a scale of 1 to 36, with 36 being the highest.

Class rank: computation denoting a student's academic position in relation to classmates. Class rank is generally reported in terms of deciles, quarters, and/or thirds. Grade point average usually determines class rank.

College: (1) a postsecondary school that offers a bachelor's degree in liberal arts or science or both, and (2) schools of a university offering the aforementioned degree programs.

College work-study program: a federally financed program that provides opportunities for students who need financial aid to work on campus or with tax-exempt employers. Work-study programs should not be confused with cooperative education programs run by many colleges to provide students with practical work experience based on their particular college major.

Deferred admission: allows an accepted student to postpone admission to college for 1 year.

Early admission or early entrance: procedure that admits students of unusually high ability into college courses and programs before they have completed high school.

Early action: procedure whereby students submit credentials to colleges early, usually by November 1. Unlike early decision, a student admitted under early action is not obligated to enroll.

Early decision: procedure that gives special consideration to a student who applies for admission by a specified date. If admitted under early decision, the student has an obligation to attend that school. The student may not accept an offer of admission from another institution at a later date.

Expected family contribution: the amount that an accrediting agency estimates that a student's family should be able to contribute toward his or her education. The amount takes into account parent resources, the student's savings, the family's earnings, and the student's earnings.

Family financial statement: a financial aid application form required by colleges using the ACT assessment for admissions purposes.

Federal Stafford Loans: government subsidized and unsubsidized (you pay the interest), low-interest loans made to students by credit unions, commercial banks, or savings and loan institutions. Repayment of a subsidized loan is guaranteed by the federal government. The amount that students may borrow and the number of years they have to repay it vary from year to year.

Free Application for Federal Student Aid (FAFSA): government need-analysis form that determines the expected family contribution and Pell Grant eligibility.

Grant: the portion of a financial aid package that the student does not have to repay.

Grade point average (GPA): number usually computed by giving quality points to each letter grade (for academic and nonacademic courses) earned during high school and then dividing by the number of earned credits. Some school systems "weigh" honors or Advanced Placement (AP) courses by awarding an extra fraction of a point to the course. Colleges frequently recalculate a student's GPA to reflect only his or her academic courses.

High school profile, course description, or transcript supplement: provides information to colleges about the high school's program of studies, grading system, and make-up of the student body. The meaning of a student's transcript (grades) is partially explained by an effective pro-

189

file that includes the percentage of students who go to 4-year colleges, the nature of the courses offered, and the grading scale. When a course title does not clearly reflect the rigor and significance of an academic course, an explanation should accompany the school profile and student transcript.

Liberal arts: academic disciplines such as mathematics, science, language, history, literature, and philosophy. These programs are designed not to prepare a student for a profession but for the development of intellectual ability and judgment.

Merit-based awards and scholarships: scholarships awarded by colleges and outside agencies on the basis of student accomplishment, rather than financial need. Merit scholarships may be awarded on the basis of a student's PSAT scores and the results of the National Merit Scholarship competition. Some merit-based awards target students of different backgrounds, cultures, and races.

Needs-based scholarships and awards: awarded on the basis of *demonstrated* financial need. You must submit personal family financial information to prove your need.

Official transcript: academic profile of the student. Transcripts should include a list of courses taken each year (including courses in progress), the rigor of those courses (AP, honors, accelerated), grades assigned for each course, GPA, and class rank (including how the rank is determined).

Parent loan for undergraduate students: primarily a loan for parents of dependent students. Loans are made directly to parents.

Pell Grants: grants given under a federal program for extremely needy families. Grants under this program ranged from $400 to $4,400 as of 2005.

Perkins Loan: a low-interest loan for students with demonstrated need. Students do not apply directly for a Perkins Loan; funds are paid directly to colleges by the federal government for allocation to students whom the colleges select.

PIN: personal identification number used to complete the online FAFSA. Both student and parent must apply for a PIN.

Preliminary SAT°/National Merit Scholarship Qualifying Test (PSAT/NMSQT): a 2-hour version of the SAT. The PSAT is a screening mechanism for the National Merit Scholarship competition. In order to be considered, students must take the test in the fall of 11th grade and score in the top 5% of students in their state. The PSAT is similar to the SAT and is therefore a good preliminary indicator of the student's potential SAT score. PSAT scores are also used for the National Merit Hispanic Scholarship and the National Achievement Scholarship Program for Outstanding Negro Students.

Profile: designed by the college scholarship service for participating colleges and scholarship awarding foundations. You must register and complete this form online. Profile requires the same basic data as FAFSA, with extra questions about assets, expenses, and resources.

Quarter system: divides the 9-month academic year into three equal parts of approximately 12 weeks each. Summer sessions are usually the same length. Credits are granted as quarter hours (3 quarter hours = 2 semester hours).

Regular admission: admission to a college in the usual manner. Students must submit an application by a specified date, and a decision is made by the college after it has received most of its applications (approximately February 15 to April 15). All applicants are informed at about the same time, although this varies with the college.

Reserve Officers' Training Corps (ROTC): students take part in training for a career in the military; tuition, books, and fees are subsidized by the military; and the student also receives a stipend to help cover personal expenses. Upon graduation, students receive a commission in the military service. Students may be obligated to serve a specified number of years in the military after graduation.

Reserve Officers' Training Corps (ROTC) scholarship: a scholarship and educational program offered by the U.S. mili-

191

tary. In return for scholarship aid, students are obligated to serve for a period of years on active duty or reserve status in one of the military services.

Rolling admission: admission to a college whereby students may submit an application at any time during the year. The college makes a decision within a few weeks of receiving the application and transcript.

SAT: a nearly 4-hour-long test divided into three sections: verbal, mathematics, and a writing exercise. Scores are reported on a scale of 200 to 800 in each section. A perfect score is 2400.

SAT or ACT preparatory courses: courses taken to prepare a student for the SAT or ACT tests.

SAT Subject Tests: one-hour tests similar to final examinations in a variety of academic subjects such as mathematics, science, history, language, literature, and writing. Subject tests are designed to measure the extent and depth of a student's knowledge of the subject.

Semester system: divides the academic year into two equal segments of approximately 18 weeks each. Summer sessions are shorter, but they require more intensive study.

Single choice early action (SCEA): also referred to as nonbinding early decision. Similar to early decision, if a student applies to a SCEA college, the student is prohibited from applying either early decision or early action to other colleges, but may apply regular admission anywhere else. Like early action, students are not bound to attend the SCEA college if they are accepted.

Student aid report: report indicates the expected family contribution and whether or not a student is eligible for a Pell Grant.

Supplemental educational opportunity grant: grant designed to provide additional support for Pell Grants based on student need. Money is paid directly to colleges to give to needy students.

Trimester system: divides the calendar year into three segments, thereby creating a continuous academic calendar of three semesters, each approximately 18 weeks in length. Credits are usually granted in semester hours.

University: a postsecondary school consisting of teaching and research facilities comprising a graduate school or professional schools. Universities offer master's degrees and doctorates, as well as undergraduate degrees.

References

ACT Inc. (n.d.a). *Frequently asked questions about the ACT writing test.* Retrieved October 22, 2005, from http://www.act.org/aap/writing/highschool/faq.html#8

ACT Inc. (n.d.b). *The ACT writing test.* Retrieved October 22, 2005, from http://www.act.org/aap/writing/index.html

Americans with Disabilities Act, 42 U.S.C. §§ 12102 et seq. (1990).

Barrow, L., & Rouse, C. E. (2005). *Does college still pay?* Retrieved December 5, 2005, from http://www.bepress.com/ev/vol2/iss4/art3

Baum, S. (1990). *Gifted but learning disabled: A puzzling paradox.* Reston, VA: ERIC Clearinghouse on Disabilities and Gifted Education. (ERIC Document Reproduction Service No. ED321484)

Baum, S., & Payea, K. (2004). *Education pays: The benefits of higher education for individuals and society.* New York: College Entrance Examination Board.

Berkner, L., Berker, A., Rooney, K., & Peter, K. (2003). *Student financing of undergraduate education: 1999–2000.* Retrieved December 1, 2005, from http://nces.ed.gov/programs/quarterly/vol_4/4_3/4_2.asp

Berkner, L., Wei, C. C., He, S., Lew, S., Cominole, M., & Siegel, P. (2005). *2003–04 national postsecondary student aid study (NPSAS:04): Undergraduate financial aid estimates for 2003–04 by type of institution (NCES 2005–163).* Retrieved December 1, 2005, from http://nces.ed.gov/pubsearch/pubsinfo.asp?pubid=2005163

Boyd, L. (1999). *I.B. or not I.B.? That is the question.* Retrieved October 25, 2005, from http://www.afsa.org/fsj/Dec99/boyd.cfm

Clinton, W. J. (1997). *Opening wide the doors of college. President Clinton's call to action for American education in the 21st century.* Retrieved December 5, 2005, from http://www.ed.gov/updates/PresEDPlan/part9.html

College Board (1993). *Taking the SAT: A guide to taking the Scholastic Assessment Test and the Test of Standard Written English.* New York: Author.

College Board (n.d.a). *Meet the SAT: What it means to your child.* Retrieved August 1, 2005, from http://www.collegeboard.com/parents/article/0,3708,700-702-0-21295,00.html

College Board (n.d.b). *SAT reasoning test.* Retrieved October 22, 2005, from http://www.collegeboard.com/student/testing/sat/about/SATI.html

College Board (n.d.c). *SAT welcome.* Retrieved October 22, 2005, from http://www.collegeboard.com/prof/counselors/tests/sat/news.html

College Board (n.d.d). *Trends in college pricing 2005.* Retrieved December 1, 2005, from http://www.collegeboard.com/prod_downloads/press/cost05/trends_college_pricing_05.pdf

College Board AP Central (n.d.). *Setting credit and placement policy.* Retrieved on October 30, 2005, from http://apcentral.collegeboard.com/colleges/setting_policy/0,,154-179-0-0,00.html

Delisle, J. R., & Berger, S. (1990). *Underachieving gifted students.* Reston, VA: ERIC Clearinghouse on Disabilities and Gifted Education. (ERIC Document Reproduction Service No. ED321483)

Duke University Talent Identification Program. (2005). *Advanced Placement teachers manuals.* Retrieved October 28, 2005, from http://www.tip.duke.edu/resources/AP_manuals

Feynman, R. (1985). *Surely you're joking, Mr. Feynman! Adventures of a curious character.* New York: W. W. Norton.

Frome, P., & Dunham, C. (2002, April). *Influence of school practices on students' academic choices.* Retrieved December 1, 2005, from http://www.sreb.org/programs/MiddleGrades/publications/reports/Guidance_Research_Brief_4-30-021.pdf

Gross, J. (2002). *Steps to college: The waiting game.* Retrieved October 22, 2005, from http://www.nacac.com/p&s_steps_0301waiting.html

Guernsey, L. (2005). *College.edu.* Alexandria, VA: Octameron Associates.

Hansen, R. (n.d.). *Are summer college prep or academic enrichment camps right for you?* Retrieved October 22, 2005, from http://www.quintcareers.com/college_prep_camps.html

Holland, J. L. (1962). Some explorations of a theory of vocational choice: One- and two-year longitudinal studies. *Psychological Monographs, 76*(26, Whole No. 545).

Individuals with Disabilities Education Act, 20 U.S.C. §1401 et seq. (1990).

Janos, P. M., & Robinson, N. M. (1985). Psychosocial development in intellectually gifted children. In F. Horowitz & M. O'Brien (Eds.), *The gifted and talented: Developmental perspectives* (pp. 149–197). Washington, DC: American Psychological Association.

Johns Hopkins University. (n.d.). *Talent loss: Why so many of the country's top-achieving low-income students never go to college.* Retrieved August 1, 2005, from http://www.jhu.edu/news_info/news/home99/mar99/talent.html

Johns Hopkins University Center for Talented Youth. (n.d.a). *History/Mission.* Retrieved August 1, 2005, from http://www.cty.jhu.edu/about/history.html

Johns Hopkins University Center for Talented Youth. (n.d.b). *Links to academic competitions.* Retrieved January 9, 2005, from http://www.jhu.edu/~gifted/imagine/linkB.htm

Karnes, F., & Riley, T. (2005). *Competitions for talented kids: Win scholarships, big prize money, and recognition.* Waco, TX: Prufrock Press.

Kaufmann, F. (1981). The 1964–1968 presidential scholars: A follow-up study. *Exceptional Children, 48,* 164–169.

Kaufmann, F., Harrel, G., Milam, C. P., Woolverton, N., & Miller, J. (1986). The nature, role, and influence of mentors in the lives of gifted adults. *Journal of Counseling and Development, 64,* 576–578.

Kestler, J., & Florman, B. (2004). *The new SAT.* New York: Spark Publishing.

Leider, A. (2005). *The A's and B's of academic scholarships* (25th ed.). Alexandria, VA: Octameron Associates.

Leider, A., & Leider, R. (2005). *Don't miss out: The ambitious student's guide to financial aid* (30th ed.). Alexandria, VA: Octameron Associates.

Mathews, J. (2005, November 24). At long last, Advanced Placement is a subject in itself. *The Washington Post Fairfax Extra,* p. VA08.

Meltzer, T., Maier, C., Brown, C., Doherty, J., Friedman, A., & Franek, R. (Eds.). (2006). *The best 361 colleges.* Princeton, NJ: The Princeton Review.

Mollison, A. (2006). *Surviving a midlife crisis.* Retrieved December 1, 2005, from http://www.educationnext.org/20061/34.html

National Association for College Admission Counseling. (2001, September). *Definitions of admission decision options.* Retrieved August 1, 2005, from http://www.nacac.com/downloads/policy_admission_options.pdf

National Association for College Admission Counseling. (2004a). *State of college admission.* Retrieved August 1, 2005, from http://www.nacac.com/research_trends.html

National Association for College Admission Counseling. (2004b). *NACAC 2004 early decision/early action guide.* Retrieved August 1, 2005, from http://www.nacac.com/downloads/04edea_guide.pdf

National Association for College Admission Counseling. (2005). *State of college admission.* Retrieved August 1, 2005, from http://www.nacacnet.org/MemberPortal/Professional Resources/Research/SOCA.htm

National Association of Secondary School Principals & National Honor Society. (n.d.). *Student contests and activities.* Retrieved January 9, 2005, from http://www.nhs.us/s_nhs/sec.asp?TRACKID=&CID=116&DID=5260

National Center for Education Statistics. (2000). *College quality and the earnings of recent college graduates.* Retrieved August 1, 2005, from http://nces.ed.gov/pubsearch/pubsinfo.asp?pubid=2000043

National Collegiate Athletic Association. (2005). *Guide for the college-bound student-athlete.* Indianapolis, IN: Author.

Olszewski-Kubilius, P. (1995). *Thinking about early entrance to college.* Retrieved August 1, 2005, from http://www.ctd.northwestern.edu/resources/earlyentrance/thinkingearly.html

Plank, S. B., & Jordan, W. J. (2001). Effects of information, guidance, and actions on postsecondary destinations: A study of talent loss. *American Educational Research Journal, 38,* 947–979.

Reis, S., & McCoach, D. B. (2002). Underachievement in gifted students. In M. Neihart, S. Reis, N. Robinson, & S. Moon (Eds.), *The social and emotional development of gifted children: What do we know?* (pp. 81–90). Waco, TX: Prufrock Press.

Rimm, S. (1986). *The underachievement syndrome: Causes and cures.* Watertown, WI: Apple.

Robinson, N., & Davidson Institute for Talent Development (2005). *Considering the options: A guidebook for investigating early college entrance—Student version* (pp. 31–32). Retrieved December 1, 2005, from http://print.ditd.org/young_scholars/ Guidebooks/YSGuidebook_Early_College_Students_12_08_ 05.pdf

Roosevelt, E. (1958). *The autobiography of Eleanor Roosevelt.* New York: HarperCollins.

Rowe, I. (2005, May). *Making college a reality for all: A submission for strengthening America's democracy.* Retrieved August 1, 2005, from http://www.pacefunders.org/pdf/essays/ Rowe%20FINAL.pdf

Rudner, L. (1999). *The scholastic achievement of home school students.* Reston, VA: ERIC Clearinghouse on Assessment and Evaluation. (ERIC Document Reproduction Service No. ED435709)

Savingforcollege.com. (n.d.a). *Intro to ESAs (Coverdell education savings accounts).* Retrieved December 1, 2005, from http:// www.savingforcollege.com/intro_to_esas

Savingforcollege.com (n.d.b). *Intro to 529s.* Retrieved December 1, 2005, from http://www.savingforcollege.com/intro_to_529s

Simpson, R. G., & Kaufmann, F. A. (1981). Career education for the gifted. *Journal of Career Education, 8,* 39–45.

Supplee, P. L. (1990). *Reaching the gifted underachiever.* New York: Teachers College Press.

Thorndike, R. L., & Hagan, E. (1986). *Measurement and evaluation in psychology and education.* New York: Macmillan.

U.S. Census Bureau. (2004). *Table 1. Earnings of year-round, full-time workers by selected characteristics: 1999.* Retrieved October 28, 2005, from http://ask.census.gov

U.S. Department of Education. (2004). *Why go to college?* Retrieved August 1, 2005, from http://studentaid.ed.gov/students/ attachments/siteresources/college.pdf

West, T. (1997). *In the mind's eye: Visual thinkers, gifted people with dyslexia and other learning difficulties, computer images and the ironies of creativity.* New York: Prometheus.

Whitmore, J. R. (1980). *Giftedness, conflict, and underachievement.* Boston: Allyn & Bacon.

Whitmore, J. R. (1986). Understanding a lack of motivation to excel. *Gifted Child Quarterly, 30,* 66–69.

Willard-Holt, C. (1999). *Dual exceptionalities.* Reston, VA: ERIC Clearinghouse on Disabilities and Gifted Education. (ERIC Document Reproduction Service No. ED430344)

Willis, G. (2005). *Saving for college. 5 tips: Getting started on the road to college.* Retrieved August 10, 2005, from http://money.cnn.com/2005/08/10/pf/saving/willis_tips/index.htm?cnn=yes

Appendix A: Early Entrance College Programs

Bard High School Early College (BHSEC)
525 East Houston Street
New York NY 10002
Phone: (212) 955-8479
http://www.bard.edu/bhsec
Open to all New York City residents who are entering either the 9th or 10th grade, BHSEC offers highly motivated students the opportunity to complete high school and the first 2 years of college, earning an associate degree, as well as a high school diploma in 4 years.

The Davidson Academy of Nevada
Davidson Institute for Talent Development
9665 Gateway Drive, Ste. B
Reno, NV 89521
Phone (775) 852-3483
http://www.davidsonacademy.unr.edu
In 2006, the Davidson Academy, a university school for profoundly gifted pupils, will open its doors to 30 profoundly gifted middle and high school students. When students have earned their Davidson Academy high school diploma, they will have the opportunity to become fully matriculated students of the University of Nevada, Reno, enrolled in the university's Honors Program.

Early Entry Program (EEP)

California State University
Los Angeles, CA 90032
Phone: (323) 343-2287
http://www.calstatela.edu/academic/eep
The Early Entrance Program for extraordinarily gifted young students allows qualified students as young as 11 years old the opportunity to excel at the university level. The average entering age is approximately 13.5 years and all EEP students must be admitted before their 16th birthday. The program maintains approximately 135 full-time highly gifted teenage students on the university's campus.

Resident Honors Program (RHP)

University of Southern California
3454 Trousdale Parkway, CAS 200
Los Angeles, CA 90089
Phone: (213) 740-2961
http://www.usc.edu/dept/LAS/general_studies/RHP/more info.htm
The Resident Honors Program at the University of Southern California is a 1-year early-entrance program for students who have exhausted high school curricula and are capable of college-level work. Students earn a high school diploma while concurrently enrolled in USC classes.

Advanced Academy of Georgia

State University of West Georgia, Honors House
Carrollton, GA 30118
Phone: (678) 839-6249
http://www.advancedacademy.org
The Advanced Academy is a residential, early-entrance-to-college program for gifted and talented high school-aged students. Students generally apply during their sophomore or junior year, but the academy also occasionally accepts younger, high-ability students. Students earn concurrent high school and college credit.

Georgia Academy of Math, Engineering, and Science (GAMES)
Middle Georgia College
1100 Second Street, SE
Cochran, GA 31014
Phone: (478) 934-3471
http://web2.mgc.edu/natsci/games/gameshome.html
Selected high school juniors or seniors with a special interest in mathematics, engineering, science, and allied health fields take courses at Middle Georgia College. Students who complete the 2-year program are given an associate's degree and a high school diploma, and are classified as college juniors.

Missouri Academy of Science, Mathematics and Computing
Northwest Missouri State University
Office of Enrollment
800 University Drive
Maryville, MO 64468-6001
Phone: (660) 562-1060
http://www.nwmissouri.edu/MASMC
Applicants must be currently enrolled in the 10th grade or its equivalent and must have completed Geometry and Algebra II by the end of their sophomore year. This is a 2-year program of college coursework, allowing students to simultaneously earn college credits and a high school diploma.

National Academy of Arts, Sciences, and Engineering (NAASE)
The Connie Belin & Jacqueline N. Blank International Center for Gifted Education and Talent Development
The University of Iowa
600 Blank Honors Center
Iowa City, IA 52242
Phone: (800) 336-6463
http://www.education.uiowa.edu/belinblank/programs/naase
Selected students who have completed coursework equivalent to the junior year in high school may accelerate their

203

academic careers and move into university research and coursework. Academy students are accepted automatically as freshmen into The University of Iowa Honors Program and live together on the honors residence hall floors. The University of Iowa also offers The Iowa Online Advanced Placement Academy for students in grades 9–12.

Simon's Rock College of Bard
84 Alford Road
Great Barrington, MA 01230
Phone: (413) 528-0771
http://www.simons-rock.edu
Simon's Rock is the nation's only accredited 4-year college of liberal arts and sciences specifically designed for younger scholars. It is a residential school. When students graduate from Simon's Rock they have either an associate's degree or a bachelor's degree. Most students enter Simon's Rock after completing the 10th or 11th grade, and follow programs leading to degrees in liberal arts. The Acceleration to Excellence Program (AEP) offers approximately 20 students per year a merit scholarship covering the full cost of tuition for the 2-year associate's degree program. The AEP also offers up to 30 partial scholarships. Simon's Rock is not strictly a school for the gifted and may be suitable for other highly motivated students.

The Clarkson School
Clarkson University
8 Clarkson Avenue
Potsdam, NY 13699
Phone: (315) 268-4425
http://www.clarkson.edu/tcs
The Clarkson School's Early Admission Program is designed primarily as a 1-year residential program for 12th-grade students. Each year, 55 to 80 talented students who have completed 11th grade and have demonstrated high interest and excellence in their academic work are selected for admission. In special cases, students in other grade levels are considered for admission. The Clarkson School community

provides a strong, supportive environment for students, who live in their own residence hall, and who enjoy an array of field trips and social activities.

Texas Academy of Mathematics and Science (TAMS)
University of North Texas
TAMS Marquis Hall 114
1511 W. Mulberry
Denton, TX 76201
Phone: (800) 241-TAMS
http://www.tams.unt.edu
The Texas Academy of Mathematics and Science is a residential program for high-school-aged Texas students who are high achievers and interested in mathematics and science and have completed 10th grade. While living on campus, students in this 2-year program complete a rigorous academic curriculum of college coursework at the University of North Texas (UNT). Upon completion, students receive a special high school diploma and are classified as college juniors.

Texas Academy of Leadership in the Humanities (TAHL)
Lamar University
P.O. Box 10062
Beaumont, TX 77710
Phone: (409) 839-2995
http://dept.lamar.edu/taolith
The Texas Academy for Leadership in the Humanities is a 2-year residential honors program that allows juniors and seniors in high school to complete their last 2 years of high school credits and their first 2 years of college requirements concurrently, while taking only college courses. This means that a student completes the program with a high school diploma and 60 or more college hours. With Advanced Placement Exams and course opportunities, it is possible for Academy students to graduate from high school with even more college hours.

205

The Program for the Exceptionally Gifted (PEG)
Mary Baldwin College (women only)
Staunton, VA 24401
Phone: (540) 887-7039
http://www.mbc.edu/peg
The Program for the Exceptionally Gifted offers young, academically talented women the opportunity to complete college during their high school years while living in a fully supervised residence hall with their true peers on the campus of Mary Baldwin College. Prospective PEG students are eligible to apply from their eighth-grade year on and are accepted based upon giftedness, consistent academic achievement, and personal maturity.

**University of Washington Transition School
and Early Entrance Program**
University of Washington
Halbert & Nancy Robinson Center for the Study of Capable Youth
Guthrie Annex II, Box 351630
Seattle, WA 98195
Phone: (206) 543-4160
http://depts.washington.edu/cscy
The Transition School, for students no more than 14 years old, and Early Entrance Program, for full-time university students who are "graduates" of the Transition School, provide the opportunity for younger students to work at a challenging level. The Transition School enables students to move from their former school setting to the University of Washington with the skills and maturity needed for a university education. As students are ready, they take one or more progressively challenging university courses along with their Transition School work until they are ready for the challenge of full-time university enrollment. The Web site also includes scholarly articles about early entrance in PDF format.

Appendix B: College Planning Web Resources

Acceleration

A Nation Deceived: How Schools Hold Back America's Brightest Students
http://nationdeceived.org

Career Interests

Career Development Manual
http://www.cdm.uwaterloo.ca

The Princeton Review Career Quiz
http://www.princetonreview.com/cte/quiz/career_quiz1.asp

What Can I Do With A Major In . . . ?
http://www.uncwil.edu/stuaff/career/Majors

College Finding/Planning Internet Sites

The Admissions Office
http://www.theadmissionsoffice.com

Campus Tours (virtual tour guide)
http://www.campustours.com

College Board Online
http://www.collegeboard.com

CollegeNet
http://www.collegenet.com

College Profiles
http://www.collegeprofiles.com

Essay Wizard
http://www.essaywizard.net

My College Guide
http://www.mycollegeguide.org

The National Association for College Admission Counseling
http://www.nacacnet.org

The National Study of School Evaluation
http://www.nsse.org

Peterson's
http://www.petersons.com

Princeton Review
http://www.princetonreview.com

Students Review
http://www.studentsreview.com

The University of Texas (link to U.S. colleges and universities)
http://www.utexas.edu/world/univ

U.S. News & World Report **School Rankings**
http://www.usnews.com/usnews/edu/college/rankings/rankindex_brief.php

University and College Directory
http://www.university-directory.org

Financial Aid

College Funding Coaches
http://www.collegefundingcoaches.com

FastWEB
http://fastweb.monster.com

The Financial Aid Information Page
http://www.finaid.org

Findtuition.com
http://www.findtuition.com

The Illinois Student Assistance Commission
http://www.collegezone.com

Octameron Associates
http://www.octameron.com

Scholarship Resource Network Express
http://www.srnexpress.com

Sallie Mae
http://www.salliemae.com

U.S. Department of Education—Find and Pay for College, Locators and Lists
http://www.ed.gov/students/college/locate/edpicks.jhtml?src=sm

209

U.S. Department of Education—Student Financial Assistance Programs
http://www.fafsa.ed.gov

Homeschooling Resources

Home School Legal Defense Association
http://www.hslda.org

Colleges That Admit Homeschoolers
http://learninfreedom.org/colleges_4_hmsc.html

Colleges With Homeschool Admission Policies Online
http://homeschooling.gomilpitas.com/olderkids/College
HSpages.htm

SAT and ACT Test Preparation

ACT, Inc.
http://www.act.org

College Board SAT Prep
http://www.collegeboard.com/student/testing/sat/prep_
one/prep_one.html

Educational Testing Service (ETS)
http://www.ets.org

EduPrep
http://www.eduprep.com/SAT_ACT.asp

Kaplan Education Center
http://www.kaptest.com

Princeton Review
http://www.princetonreview.com/college

SAT Power Tactics by Barnes & Noble
http://www.sparknotes.com/testprep/newsat/powertactics

SAT Subject Test Requirements
http://www.ivywest.com/satiireq.htm

Testprep—Triumph College Admissions
http://www.testprep.com

Study Skills

Study Guides and Strategies
http://www.studygs.net

Center for Advancement of Learning at Muskingum
http://muskingum.edu/home/cal

Virginia Tech Study Skills Self-Help Information
http://www.ucc.vt.edu/stdysk/stdyhlp.html

Talent Searches

Center for Talent Development at Northwestern University
http://www.ctd.northwestern.edu

Center for Talented Youth at Johns Hopkins University
http://www.jhu.edu/gifted

Talent Identification Program at Duke University
http://www.tip.duke.edu

Rocky Mountain Talent Search at the University of Denver
http://www.du.edu/education/ces/rtms.hml

Appendix C: SAT and ACT Hints and Resources

SATs: Hints, Tips, and Resources

What do SAT preparatory courses have to do with gifted students? The College Board (1993) says, "The SAT measures *developed* verbal and mathematical reasoning abilities. . . . Short-term drills and cramming are likely to have little effect. . . . Your abilities are related to the time and effort spent" (p. 4).

On that basis, many gifted students are already well-prepared for their SATs. They take challenging courses and generally do extensive outside reading, the best preparation possible for the exam.

Despite claims to the contrary, however, evidence gathered over the past 10 years suggests that SAT scores can be raised significantly through careful preparation. As educators have become more knowledgeable about the SAT and copies of the tests have become readily available, sophisticated preparatory programs have appeared.

To Prep or Not to Prep?

Some gifted students have very strong mathematical talents and weaker verbal skills, while others have just the reverse. Both of these types of students may score well on one part of the test, but do poorly on the other. Thus, they may need help to raise their scores in the weaker area. Many gifted students are highly competitive and hate to leave an answer blank on a test. But, there is a .25 point penalty for every wrong answer on the SAT. The penalty is designed to eliminate any gain you may get from random guesses, so, is it better to leave a blank? Probably not. There's a difference between randomly guessing among five items on a multiple-choice question, and narrowing your choices before you guess. For example, if you can narrow your choices down to 2 or 3, or even 4 of the 5 choices, you will increase the odds of making a correct guess. According to *The New SAT*, (Kestler & Florman, 2004), if you can eliminate even one answer choice you should always guess. An exception occurs in the grid-in mathematical questions; that is, problems that are answered by marking an answer in ovals on a provided grid. There is no penalty for incorrect answers to these problems. However, the odds of guessing the right answer on the grid-in problems is pretty small. Some gifted students are highly creative. However, the same characteristic that makes gifted students creative problem solvers may cause difficulty when the student has to choose exactly one correct answer. Gifted students often find reasons why more than one answer could be correct. For example, in a well-publicized case, a student solved a mathematical problem by (mentally) putting one figure inside the other, instead of abutting two sides. As a result, his answer made better sense than the one prescribed.

214

Many small- to medium-sized private colleges offer scholarships on the basis of SAT scores. These colleges are listed in *The A's and B's: Your Guide to Academic Scholarships* (Leider, 2005). In addition, some colleges offer students the option to skip first-level English courses in composition based on their SAT scores.

Some students prepare for the SAT to overcome test anxiety. Practice can help, because pages of the test will then look familiar and the student will not have to read every word of the instructions. If the student takes supervised practice tests and sees his or her scores rise over a period of time, a positive attitude will develop. If you want to encourage your teen to practice, Kaplan, the test preparation company, has one answer—software that runs on hand-held computers, cell phones, and smart phones. The Kaplan Mobile programs are available online from Handmark (see http://handmark.com), which developed the software, or at electronics stores.

Should gifted students prepare for the PSAT? Students are generally advised to take the PSAT without advance preparation. Their scores will help them decide whether or not they should prepare for the SAT. However, if a student is an anxious test taker, poor performance on the PSAT could increase that anxiety when the time comes to take the SAT. Most high schools will allow 10th-grade students to take to take the PSAT for practice. The scores then would help the student decide whether or not to prepare for the 11th-grade administration of the test.

There are many preparatory courses, ranging in price from less than $200 to more than $1,600. To evaluate an SAT prep course, ask the following questions:

- Are actual SATs used as practice tests in the course?
- Are students held accountable for homework?
- Are content and technique both treated?
- Who teaches the course?

The strength of the teaching staff and the motivation of the student make a huge difference. Teachers need to be a combination of coach and cheerleader, as well as knowledgeable about content and technique. The student needs to know why she or he is there and must be willing to put in the daily time to succeed. Career centers and guidance offices often have lists of prep companies and/or applications and may make recommendations. Talk to students who have taken such courses for firsthand information. Some students overemphasize SAT and ACT test scores. Avoid this mistake by knowing the way the scores are used by the colleges to which you intend to apply.

What kind of improvement can you expect? Most program directors will quote averages for their courses. Beware of guarantees. Very low and very high scores on previous tests usually mean the students will not increase as much as those with middling scores. Better scorers tend to make their greatest increases early in a course, because content is not as big a factor for them as technique. Rarely, will a "prepped" student's scores decrease. Other students will go up 50 to 100 points with no prepping between tests.

About the SAT Reasoning Test

The SAT Reasoning Test measures critical reading, mathematical reasoning, and writing skills that students have developed over time that they need to be successful in college. The critical reading section, formerly known as the verbal section, will include short reading passages along with the existing longer reading passages. Reading passages will range from 500 to 800 words. The new short reading passages will be paragraphs of about 100 words, followed by questions similar to questions on the longer reading passages.

In addition, there is one 25-minute unscored section, known as the variable or equating section. This unscored section may be either a critical reading, math, or multiple-choice writing section. This unscored section does not count toward the final score, but is used to try out new questions for future editions of the SAT and to ensure that scores on new editions of the SAT are comparable to scores on earlier editions of the test.

The SAT consists of nine sections, including a 25-minute essay, each timed separately. The essay will always be the first section of the SAT, and the 10-minute multiple-choice writing section will always be the final section. The other 25-minute sections can appear in any order, as can the two 20-minute sections. Test takers sitting next to each other in the same testing session may have test books with rearranged sections.

According to the College Board, the current SAT is better aligned than previous versions with current curriculum and institutional practices in high school and college (College Board, n.d.c). By including a third measure of skills, writing, the SAT reinforces the importance of writing throughout a student's education and will help colleges make better admissions and placement decisions. Students can practice for the writing section using sample essay prompts found on the College Board's Web site. Each section of the SAT is scored on a scale of 200–800 for a possible total of 2400 (College Board, n.d.c).

The ACT: Hints, Tips, and Resources

Much of the information on SATs also applies to ACTs, so even if you are not taking the SATs, read the previous section on that test.

The ACT is a standardized test preferred by some colleges. It is structured differently than the SAT. There are four multiple-choice academic areas, plus the newly added and optional 30-minute writing section: (1) English, which measures standard written English and rhetorical skills; (2) Mathematics, which measures mathematical skills students have typically acquired in courses taken up to the beginning of grade 12; (3) Reading, which measures reading comprehension; and (4) Science, which measures the interpretation, analysis, evaluation, reasoning, and problem-solving skills required in the natural sciences (ACT, n.d.a). The writing section measures writing skills emphasized in high school English classes and in entry-level college composition courses (ACT, n.d.a). Unlike the SAT, the score on each section is based solely on the number of questions answered correctly; there is no penalty for guessing. It is to your advantage to answer every question even if you must guess. Some strategies for taking the tests include (ACT, n.d.a):

217

- Familiarize yourself with the content of the ACT tests by taking practice tests. Some gifted students have a tendency to breeze by the instructions without focusing. The instructions on every test are very important if you are going to be successful. For example, the ACT English, reading, and science tests ask for the "best" answer, while the math test asks for the "correct" answer. So one of the choices on the math test is "correct," while the choices on the other tests may be all correct, depending on your interpretation, and require some thinking to determine the "best" answer. Directions for the writing test are also very important. The directions spell out the aspects of writing that will be evaluated. They also tell you where in the test booklet you can write to *plan* your essay, and where you can write the final version.

- Learn to pace yourself. For example, on the mathematics test, which consists of 60 multiple-choice questions, one possibility is to simply divide the amount of time available for the test by the number of questions you'll have to answer. One problem with this is that you may come up with a length of time that doesn't mean much. Do you have any clear idea of how long 80 seconds is, for example? Try dividing the questions in groups, by type, and figure out how much time to spend on each group. On the English, reading, and science tests, you can pace yourself by figuring out a certain amount of time to spend reading each passage and then determining how much time you have left to spend on the associated questions. For example, if you have four passages to cover in 40 minutes, you would allow yourself roughly 10 minutes for each passage and the related questions. For the writing test, pace yourself in the way that best suits your personal writing strategy. You won't have enough time to fully draft, revise, and then recopy your essay. So, take a few minutes to plan.

- Read carefully and thoughtfully. Some students read so quickly that they miss important phrases or words. Make sure you know exactly what the question asks. In practice sessions, try to turn the question around and then see if the answer changes. Look for words such as *not* or *least;* pay attention to qualifying words such as *always, usually, seldom,* and so forth. Read all the answer choices before selecting one.

- Decide on a strategy for changing your mind. People may tell you to always go with your original answer when you think you might have marked the wrong answer. However, some research by testing specialists suggests that you should change your answer when you change your mind. So what should you do? It depends on you and your testing style; there are no easy answers. Before you change an answer, think about how you approached the question. Ask yourself why you thought one answer was better than the other, and then changed your mind. Don't change answers arbitrarily.

- Check your work—unless you think that checking your work will cause anxiety or conflict. You know your own style. If you aren't sure, be sure to take enough practice tests so that you know whether or not to second guess yourself.

- Don't panic. Take your time, and pause to breathe if you feel anxious. When you get your results, if you think you can do better, take the test again. Three test-taking sessions should be your maximum, unless there is a wide variance between your scores. In that case, you can take it a fourth time.

Appendix D: Junior Year Planning Checklist

The following calendar of college planning steps is a detailed checklist you can use to make sure you are on target for 11th and 12th grades:

___ Prepare a college planning portfolio that includes academic courses (including courses taken during the summer or after school), extracurricular activities, community service, achievements, and awards.

___ Make up a chart that can be used to keep track of dates and details. Your chart should include:

    ___ application deadlines (including early action and early decision dates);

    ___ financial aid deadlines (they are often different at different colleges);

    ___ notification dates;

    ___ tests required;

    ___ costs;

    ___ number and type of recommendations required;

    ___ interview deadlines and locations; and

    ___ dates for ACTS, SATs, and subject tests.

___ Save your writing samples. Some colleges ask to see all of the drafts, as well as the final product.

___ Develop a list of 10 to 20 colleges. Work up a comparison chart. Include factors that are important to you, and keep in mind the following factors:

    ___ size (campus, number of students);

    ___ geographic location (urban, rural, North, South, etc.);

    ___ course offerings (Do they teach what you like?);

    ___ cost (tuition, room and board, books, travel to and from home, etc.);

    ___ available scholarships or tuition assistance programs;

    ___ extracurricular activities (newspaper, sports, etc.); and

    ___ selectivity (degree of difficulty).

___ Some additional points to consider include:

    ___ curriculum and course requirements for specific majors;

    ___ student life;

    ___ special programs (e.g., study abroad);

    ___ academic advising and career counseling procedures;

    ___ whether professors or teaching assistants teach freshman courses;

    ___ faculty-student relationships; and

    ___ student access to required readings, laboratory space, and computer terminals (e.g., Is the campus wireless? If not, are there enough terminals for everyone to use during peak periods, such as midsemester and final exams?).

___ Visit several colleges you are considering. Make sure that the colleges you want to visit will be in session, and call ahead for an appointment if you want an interview with an admissions officer.

___ Consider a summer activity such as:

    ___ local or university-based summer school (keyboarding, performing arts, computer programming, engineering, philosophy, etc.);

___ a summer internship;

___ school-sponsored travel;

___ courses offered by talent search programs (i.e., the opportunity to acquire college credits and try out a college lifestyle); or

___ a college planning seminar (offered by many colleges).

___ Ask for letters of recommendation from your supervisor, camp director, formal or informal mentor, or others before you complete your summer and school year activities. Do not wait until later. You want these people to write about you when they remember you best. Ask that the letters be addressed to "To Whom It May Concern," and give the letters to your guidance counselor as soon as possible. Keep copies.

___ Send away for application forms for 6 to 10 colleges.

___ Make appointments for personal interviews at colleges you plan to visit in the fall or winter.

___ Recheck application deadlines. Start filling out application forms early in the fall. Learn how to complete an error-free application. Make extra copies of each application form. Use the copies for practice before completing the originals.

___ Unless instructions say otherwise, type everything. If you can't type, consider using a computerized application. Have someone proofread every word on your application forms. Correct all errors.

___ Make and keep copies of everything.

Appendix E: Contests and Competitions

Humanities and Social Science Competitions

Achievement Awards in Writing
http://www.ncte.org/about/awards/student

Americanism Essay Contest
http://www.fra.org/Content/fra/AboutFRA/Essay
Contest/default.cfm

**Arts Recognition Talent Search (ARTS):
National Foundation for Advancement in the Arts**
http://www.artsawards.org

Gutenberg Awards
http://www.igaea.org

High School Communications Contest:
http://www.nfpw.org/competitions.htm

Idea of America Essay Contest
http://www.wethepeople.gov/essay

International Writing, Photo Contest
http://www.uiowa.edu/~quill-sc/Contests/contests.
html

Laws of Life Essay Contest
http://www.lawsoflife.org

"My Turn" Essay Competition
http://www.newsweekeducation.com/myturn2006

National Biblical Greek Exam
http://www.greekexam.com

National Forensic League Tournament
http://www.nflonline.org

National French Contest: "Le Grand Concours"
http://www.frenchteachers.org/concours

National Geographic Bee
http://www.nationalgeographic.com/geographybee

National German Testing and Awards Program
http://www.aatg.org/programs/hsstudentprogs/testing_
program

National History Day Contest
http://nhd.acuityweb.com/NationalContest.htm

National Latin Exam
http://www.nle.org

National Spanish Examination
http://www.2nse.org

National Spelling Bee
http://www.spellingbee.com

National Student Television Award for Excellence
http://www.nationalstudent.tv

National Peace Essay Contest
http://www.usip.org/ed/npec

Optimist International Oratorical Contest
http://www.optimist.org

Scholastic Art & Writing Awards
http://www.artandwriting.org

Voice of Democracy Scholarship Competition and Patriot's Pen Essay Contest
http://www.vfw.org

Mathematics Competitions

American Mathematics Competitions
http://www.unl.edu/amc

American Regions Mathematics League
http://arml.com

Continental Mathematics League
http://www.continentalmathleague.hostrack.com

MATHCOUNTS
http://www.mathcounts.org

Math Olympiads
http://www.moems.org

National Mathematics League Contests
http://www.mathleague.com/contests.htm

USA Mathematical Talent Search (USAMTS)
http://www.usamts.org

Science, Technology, and Engineering Competitions

227

AAPT Physics Bowl
http://www.aapt.org/Contests/physicsbowl.cfm

American Computer Science League
http://acsl.org

Christopher Columbus Awards
http://www.christophercolumbusawards.com

Discovery Channel Young Scientist Challenge (DCYSC)
http://www.sciserv.org/dcysc

Dupont Challenge Science Essay Awards Competition
http://glcomm.com/dupont/home.html

The Explorers Club Youth Activity Fund Grants
http://explorers.org/grants/grants.php

ExploraVision Awards
http://www.exploravision.org

Intel International Science and Engineering Fair
http://www.sciserv.org/isef

Intel Science Talent Search
http://www.sciserv.org/sts

International Physics Olympiads
http://www.jyu.fi/tdk/kastdk/olympiads

Junior Science and Humanities Symposium
http://www.jshs.org

Junior Engineering Technical Society (JETS)
Test of Engineering Aptitude in Math and Science (TEAMS)
http://www.jets.org/programs/teams-home.htm

National Engineering Design Challenge
http://www.jets.org/programs/nedc.cfm

Science Olympiad
http://www.soinc.org

Siemens Westinghouse Competition in Math, Science, and Technology
http://www.siemens-foundation.org

Technology Student Association Competitions
http://www.tsaweb.org

Young Astronaut Program
http://www.youngastronauts.org

Miscellaneous Competitions

Future Problem Solving Program
http://www.fpsp.org

Invent America!
http://www.inventamerica.org/contest.cfm

The Knowledge Master Open
http://www.greatauk.com/KMO.html

Questions Unlimited
http://www.qunlimited.com

National High School Chess Championship
http://www.uschess.org

Odyssey of the Mind (OM)
http://www.odysseyofthemind.com

Thinkquest
http://www.thinkquest.org

United States Academic Decathlon
http://www.usad.org

(Competitions and contests compiled from Johns Hopkins University Center for Talented Youth, n.d.b; Karnes & Riley, 2005; and National Association of Secondary School Principals and National Honor Society, n.d.)

About the Author

Sandra L. Berger has been a citizen activist and advocate for gifted children for more than 30 years. She originally was led down this path by her own gifted youngsters. Berger holds a master's degree in gifted education curriculum and instruction with training in counseling. For 15 years, she was the gifted education information specialist at the ERIC Clearinghouse on Disabilities and Gifted Education and the AskERIC system, responding to thousands of questions about gifted and special education. She is a member of the editorial advisory board and a technology columnist for *Understanding Our Gifted*, has authored numerous articles in the field of gifted education, and shares her views on college planning and gifted education through participation in national, regional, and state conferences. Berger and her husband of 46 years currently have 4 grandchildren.